ESSAYS ON ETHICS, GOVERNANCE, AND ECONOMY

TRUNG LE

LE FOUNDATION PRESS

Le Foundation Press

www.Le-Foundation.org

Copyright ©2010 by Trung Le

All rights reserved.

First Edition, Second Printing

Please contact the publisher regarding discounts available for schools, teachers, and parent/faculty organizations.

Le Foundation Press, P.O. Box 21625, San Jose, CA 95151

info@Le-Foundation.org

ISBN 978-0-557-40132-1

Printed in the United States of America

No part of this book may be reproduced without the permission of the publisher.

This book is dedicated to my mentors, to all the hard working teachers and everyone else who is doing their part to make this world a better place, and to students seeking knowledge, insight, wisdom, and fulfillment of their human potential.

TABLE OF CONTENTS

PART I: VALUE THEORY AND ETHICS

1. Plato on Human Nature in the *Republic*   3

2. Aristotle on Eudaimonia in the *Nicomachean Ethics*, Books I, II   13

3. Aristotle on Relationships in the *Nicomachean Ethics*, Books VIII, IX   25

4. The Search for Guiding Principles in Natural Law Theory   35

5. Mill and Kant on Morality   51

6. Machiavelli on the Ethics of Political Power   57

PART II: GOVERNANCE

7. Arguments in Favor and Against Strong & Centralized Government   71

8. Changes in Governance   81

9. Challenges Facing Global Civil Society   93

10. Liberal Democracy   107

PART IV: ECONOMY AND STATE INTERVENTION

11. Economic Liberalization in Vietnam   139

12. Venezuela and State Welfare   151

Part I: Value Theory and Ethics

Chapter 1:
Plato on Human Nature in the *Republic*

Introduction

Plato, in the *Republic*, not only lays out the ideal aristocratic government, but also the ideal society, down to the family structure. Before we explore Plato's political and social philosophy, we must understand his philosophy of human nature. The rule of thumb is this. If human beings are selfish and negative in other ways, then government needs to be stronger to keep people under control. This means that government needs to be centralized, strong, and aristocratic or tyrannical in order to keep selfish individuals in line, otherwise, there will be chaos and no civil society. If human beings, on the other hand, are good by nature, there is less of a need for a strong, centralized, aristocratic or tyrannical government because people are disciplined enough to control themselves. Even if people are not good, and if they are born as a blank slate, proper social conditioning, education, and laws are required to keep them in line. There is no need to constantly control people through force and manipulation. Plato believed in the former – that people are selfish, unwilling to change, are not truth seekers, are not wise, and therefore they should not be in charge of government. This is also the reason why Plato was anti-democratic. In place of democracy, he favored an elite group of philosopher-politicians called the guardians. He was also in favor of using manipulation to keep the majority of the people under control.

Plato presented three primary arguments to prove that human beings are selfish and untrustworthy by nature, and therefore are not fit to rule society. The first is based on the trial and death of his teacher, Socrates. The second is the allegory of the cave. The third is the story of the ring that makes a person invisible. Let us explore these arguments in further detail.

The First Argument: The Trial and Death of Socrates

The story of the trial and death of Socrates is based upon the state of Athens accusing Socrates for "corrupting the youth". How did it led up to his execution? Let us begin from the beginning. A friend of Socrates went to the oracle at Delphi. These oracles were so called priests that had a connection to the gods. People go to these priests to seek advice in the forms of fortunes in exchange for money. At Delphi, the friend of Socrates was told, "There is no one wiser than your friend Socrates." He then went back and recited what the oracle had said to Socrates. Socrates didn't believe it at first, and so he went out to put the statement to the test. How did he do this? He basically went around and engaged in a dialogue with various people in society to determine whether they truly know what they claim to know. He found out that he was very successful at proving that people do not truly know what they claim to know. People became curious at this philosophic approach. He eventually had followers, and among them were the sons of wealthy aristocrats. There were other people, including politicians, that didn't like what was being done. Socrates was questioning people's beliefs, the way of social life, government, and even the existence of the gods. The state eventually brought him in on the grounds of "corrupting the youth". In so many words, this meant that they didn't want him stirring up trouble. The jury system at that time was very large, consisting of several hundreds of free Greek men. The jury, by a small margin, eventually founded him guilty, and sentenced him to death by drinking hemlock.

What is interesting is the fact that at that time, the convicted criminal could offer an alternative sentence. For example, Socrates could have chosen exile. Why did he not do this? He said that it would be a shame for him to go elsewhere to live because this was his home. Furthermore, if he was exiled in another city-state, he would do the same thing – engage in philosophical debate to determine whether people knew what they claimed to have known. He feared that the same consequence might result if this were the case. While in prison awaiting his punishment, a friend of Socrates asked him, "Are you not afraid of death"? He responded that a person should not be afraid of something that he or she has not experienced yet. Socrates stated that two things can happen after death. The first is that people die, there is no afterlife, and therefore nothing happens. If this is the case, then people do not experience any pain, and will not be aware of anything at all because they cease to be conscious. In fact, once this happens, the person will not even know that he or she is dead. If this happens, Socrates says, then he doesn't mind it at all. On the other hand, if gods exists and if there is an afterlife, then we go there. In the afterlife, Socrates would also engage in philosophical debate to determine whether people in the afterlife truly know what they claim to know. It wouldn't be a surprise for him to question the gods about the afterlife either. This, he wouldn't mind either. So either way, death doesn't seem that terrible.

Socrates had many supporters. Someone could have bribed the guards to set him free. Why did Socrates chose not to do this? The reason is because he thought that the state is like our parents. They make our life possible by providing the basic necessities and managing the society that we live in. To escape from prison is to go against the state and this would be as bad as going against our parents. This is the reason why he did not escape. In the end, Socrates died by drinking hemlock, which was a poison that slowly paralyzed the entire body.

This event had a profound influence on Plato. Due to the fact that the majority of the jury believed that Socrates was guilty for "corrupting the youth" is unjustifiable according to Plato. For this reason, he concluded that people in general are not wise. They do not know how to make wise and just decisions, therefore, they are in no position to govern society. Any type of ruler would have to be wiser and more just than these juries.

The Second Argument: The Allegory of the Cave

The second story is the story of the cave. This story serves several purposes. One purpose is to describe his theory of knowledge. Another purpose is to give us more reasons to mistrust people. For the purpose of this chapter, I will focus solely on the latter.

The allegory of the cave is about a group of prisoners that are tied to a pole and forced to look in one direction. The only thing that they can see is shadows on a wall. These shadows are projected by a light source behind the prisoners - a fire. In front of the fire is a walkway that people walk across while holding various objectives over their heads. The fire casts a shadow of these objects onto the wall of the cave. This results in the prisoners believing that the shadows of these objects are the real thing because they cannot see the true cause of the shadows behind them. One day, one of the prisoners is able to free himself. He then turns around and sees the light source and the people walking on the pathway holding objects above their heads. This becomes the moment that he realizes that the shadows on the wall are not real. He then sees a light source from a tunnel that leads to the outside world. He walks through the tunnel and eventually reaches the outside of the cave. At first, his eyes hurt because they have to adjust to the bright sunlight. After his eyes finally adjust, he sees everything in the real world – the trees, the pond, the animals, the sky, the sun, etc. To realize that this is the real world is more shocking than turning around and seeing the cause of the shadows inside the cave. The freed prisoner becomes enlightened and realized that he has lived a deceitful life.

He decides that it is his moral obligation to go free the other prisoners inside the cave by telling them the truth. So he goes back inside to do so. While attempting to explain to the other prisoners what he has seen and what the true causes of the shadows were, they didn't believe him. There are several reasons for not believing in the truth. The first is that it was hard to believe in something they themselves have not experienced. The second is that they have a herd mentally and was skeptical towards the individual for believing otherwise. The third is that these prisoners feared the truth because they feared change. After all, they have been living inside this cave their entire lives and this is all they know. To believe in anything else and to change in any way might result in discomfort in the form of stress, and this is something they rather not do. Plato believed that the majority of the people in society are like these prisoners inside the cave. The majority of the people are not truth seekers, they conform to the average life, they hesitate to change, and they have a herd mentality. These are also reasons why the majority is unfit to govern society, and that it is best for them to stay where they are.

The Third Argument: The Ring

Plato tells us a third hypothetical story in the *Republic* about a ring that makes a person become invisible. If someone were to find this ring and uses it, what would such a person do with this power? I have asked this question to my students throughout my years of teaching. The number one response is to go rob a bank. Another common response was sneaking into places illegally to serve one's interests, such as sneaking into a sporting event, onto a plane to fly somewhere for free, into government agencies to gain inside information, etc. Some students said that they would play jokes on their friends to scare them. Others said that they would spy on people they know to see whether they talk about them behind their backs. Very few people said that they would use the ring to become a super hero, for example by fighting crime.

We can conclude, just like Plato did, that the majority of people, if they had this power, would use it for selfish gain. Very few people would use it to benefit society. This story further supports the argument that people are selfish because they would do things that they would not otherwise do if they had the power of invisibility. Government must keep people under control with force, and if necessary, through manipulation, in order to maintain a civil society. Who then should rule over society? Plato preferred an elite group of people called the class of the guardians.

The Guardians

Plato distinguishes between three different classes – the guardians, the auxiliary guardians (or the soldiers), and the craftsmen (everyone else). The guardians are an elite group of people in society that are trained since childhood to be the politicians and ultimately the overseers of society. The auxiliary guardians are the soldiers that are needed to protect society, both from internal and external threats, and for expansion of territory. Everyone else in society is grouped under the category of craftsmen, who are also important because they provide the goods and services for society.

The class system is justified for two primary reasons. The first is that people are born with different skills. Some are better than others in some skills and have different talents. People, therefore, are not equal by nature. This plurality of skills is beneficial to society because people, by nature, also desire a variety of goods and services to achieve the happy life. For example, Plato's explanation of the minimal city versus the luxurious city proves that people do not want to live in a basic society, doing the same things, and with access to limited goods and services. People, by nature, prefer a plurality of goods and services, such as a variety of food, a variety of clothing, jewelry, entertainment, a social life, etc. There has to be a multitude of people in society to provide for these goods and services. The class system, therefore, is partly the result of the specialization of skills. The second reason for the class system is more apparent. Plato believed that an aristocratic class who is well educated, wise, and just must govern society because the majority of the people are not fit to do so. The guardian class consists of men and women who have been raised specifically for this purpose. They are the truth seekers, they are wiser than anyone else, and they are the most rational, therefore, they know what is best for society. Due to the fact that they have been trained not to be selfish, they will rule for the sake of the people rather than to serve selfish interests like many politicians that we know of today.

How are the guardians recruited and how are they trained? Children who show signs of intelligence and the potential to become good guardians are taken away from their families at an early age. They live in a communal society sharing property, housing, and labor. They will not have any dealings with money. Growing up this will reduce the chances of them becoming selfish in the future. They will not rule for the sake of money or to acquire material things such as personal property. False stories of the gods or stories that present the gods in a negative light will be censored from poetry. They will be educated to be gentle towards their citizens and fierce towards their enemies. All must serve in war to learn the art of warfare and to show that they are courageous between the ages of 30 and 45. They will receive a well rounded liberal arts education consisting of mathematics, philosophy, gymnastics, arts, and humanities.

The family life of the guardians is also communal. Plato believed that people should not be committed to one wife or one husband because this will lead to personal preference over people that we are committed to. He wanted to set up a society where people treat everybody equally as if everyone is a member of the family. This will also reduce the amount of violence that might potentially occur if we have personal biasness towards some individuals. Plato also believed in eugenics – the breeding of superior genetic traits. For this reason, he lied to the public by telling them that the mating process is done by lottery. The reality is that there are people behind the scenes carefully selecting those with the best genetic traits to mate with one another. Children of these guardians are raised by a class of people called nurses. No one will know who his or her biological child is to further reduce personal biasness in society, and therefore, will reduce the amount of violence that might occur.

Conclusion

Through the trial and death of Socrates, the allegory of the cave, and the story of the ring, Plato concluded that the majority of human beings are selfish, have a herd mentality, are non truth seekers, are not wise, are unjust, do not like to change, and are diverse in nature with different interests, strengths, weaknesses, and talents. These are the reasons Plato believed that the majority are unfit to rule society, and therefore, a specialized class called the guardians will rule over society because they are the wise truth seekers who knows what's best for society. The use of lies, censorship, and eugenics are justified in achieving the end goal, which is to achieve complete harmony in his ideal society.

Chapter 2:
Aristotle on Eudaimonia in the *Nicomachean Ethics*
Books I, II, and X

Introduction

Aristotle devoted Book I, II, and X of the *Nicomachean Ethics* to explore the concept of eudaimonia, which is translated as human flourishing and happiness. Eudaimonia requires us to fulfill the human function, which is ultimately the act of contemplation. We can do this better than any other animal, and therefore it is unique to us. Eudaimonia also requires us to act virtuously, and for Aristotle, virtue is striving for the means between two extremes. Eudaimonia also requires that we have external goods such as money and a good family. Let us now explore in detail his philosophy on eudaimonia as it is laid out in his book, the *Nicomachean Ethics*.

The Human Function

Aristotle begins the *Nicomachean Ethics* by discussing the function of things. Eudaimonia is based upon finding and fulfilling the human function and this function is unique to us. He states:

> Presumably, however, to say that happiness is the chief good seems a platitude, and a clearer account of what it is [is] still desired. This might perhaps be given, if we could first ascertain the function of man. For just as for a flute-player, a sculptor, or any artist, and, in general, for all things that have a function or activity, the good and the 'well' is thought to reside in the function, so would it seem to be for man, if he has a function.[1]

In other words, happiness being the chief good is not an adequate definition. What exactly is the good, how can it be described, and how do we obtain it? Since it is presumed that everything has a function, Aristotle determines that the good is performing that function well. The function or activity of any artist is to perform that art well. The good flute-player plays the flute well, the good sculptor sculpts well, and so forth. These are easily definable and specific examples, but the function of a human being is more difficult to obtain. Aristotle limits his functional definition to humans and

---

[1] Barnes, J., ed. *The Complete Works of Aristotle*. Princeton: Princeton U. Press, 1984. Section 1097b23-29.

excludes that life (nutrition and growth) from being the ultimate human function. Here is his reason for doing so:

> Life seems to be common even to plants, but we are seeking what is peculiar to man. Let us exclude, therefore, the life of nutrition and growth.[2]

It is indeed true that nutrition and growth is common to all life forms. But why must Aristotle exclude life as being the functional definition, and thus, having to exclude animals and plants from the equation? Wouldn't it be better to have a universal functional definition instead of one that is limited to humans? Why should humans be placed above plants and other life forms? It seems that Aristotle doesn't want an answer that is common to all, but one that is unique to only humans, but then this would be a form of species-specific discrimination.

If we limit the definition to human beings, we will know what our function is, and therefore what the good is, but only pertaining to the human species and not to others. Aristotle concludes that:

> [The] human good turns out to be activity of soul in conformity with excellence, and if there are more than one excellence, in conformity with the best....[3]

The function of human being is living in conformity with excellence. In Chapter VIII, Book I of the *Nicomachean Ethics*, Aristotle discusses the identification of happiness as excellence, and happiness is spoken in many ways, including the idea that happiness is partly the fulfillment of pleasure and that happiness involves external goods. Living the good life is living the virtuous life, which is living in accordance of the virtues such as the virtue of courage, temperance, liberality, magnificence, and justice. All of this is in relation to the function of the human being, of how humans should live among humans. But what about other life forms? How should we live in relation to animals, plants, and to the rest of nature? It is reasonable to say that happiness and the good must also have something to do with how we live harmoniously with our environment, which is why the functional definition should not be limited to humans, but should

---

[2] Ibid., 1098a1.

[3] Ibid., 1098a16.

include the rest of nature as well. By establishing a universal definition to begin with, we can establish how to live the good life among the rest of nature. If our function is to survive, the good is how well we survive.

Why the Human Function is Not Survival

Some may argue that it would be better to have a more universal definition. Let us say that the function of living things including humans, animals, and plants is ultimately to survive. This can be observed across all life forms, from the basic bacteria to a complex organism such as a human being, across different geographical locations throughout the history of Earth. The purpose of survival is widely held and supported by evidence by psychologists, sociologist, and scientists alike. Since it is the most basic and common among humans and other life forms, we will say that the functional definition is to survive.

What are some of the reasons to support the notion that survival is the most basic and universal function? Let us examine it from a psychological and evolutionary point of view, pertaining to procreation, family and social life. The natural purpose of sex is to procreate - to continue the line of existence by passing our genes onto future generations. In addition to this natural tendency of wanting to have sex, we also do what is within our power to promote our own survival and that of our offspring. In this sense, our main and deeply rooted, natural function is to survive. This can be scientifically studied across human cultures and across the animal kingdom, throughout the history of the Earth when life first emerged. In human society such as our very own here in the United States, we work long hours to earn a living in order to afford things that promotes to our survival, such as a place to live, clothing, and food. Almost everything else that we desire is either a means to achieving this end or is due to our social conditioning to become compulsive consumers. In third world countries where poverty is extreme, families tend to be large to promote survival. It would make sense for a family living in an agricultural society to have many offspring to plow the field and harvest the crops to help bring in additional income. In East-Asian cultures such as China and Vietnam, filial piety, or having respect and taking care of elders is of utmost importance within the society. Traditional families tend to be large, with many generations living under one roof, with the younger generation taking care of the older. These would all seem to be a means to the same end, which is to fulfill the function of survival. If they fulfill their goals well, for example through filial piety, then they are performing the function of survival well.

The humanistic psychologist Abraham Maslow came up with the 'hierarchy of needs'. They are broken up into four lower-order needs of deficiency motivations and a final, advanced level involving the fulfillment of one's potential. The lowest level consists of physiological needs - needs such as air, food, and shelter, of which are necessary for survival. The second level involves safety needs, the third level is love and belonging, the fourth level involves esteem, and the fifth level is self-actualization. Each lower level need must be met before a person can move onto the next level. If a person is occupied with trying to find food and shelter to fulfill physiological needs, he or she is doing so to survive first and foremost, and not worrying about love, belongingness or about self-esteem. There is priority in the hierarchy of needs, and the primary one is to fulfill the physiological needs. These lower level needs, especially the first two levels, can be applied to the animals and plants as well because they also have these basic survival needs to fulfill. Animals hunt for food and protect their young. These survival needs among plants are less obvious unless we look at their physical structure. The large surface area of leaves allows the maximum exposure to sunlight, the stems, trunks, and roots provide strength and integrity, and they grow towards the light source, which is usually the sun, and hence grow in an upward direction.

It would seem that surviving well isn't necessary all good in the sense of being free of pain because surviving, as stated in the theory of evolution, is survival of the fittest, which may or may not involve conflict and violence among other life forms to increase the chance of survival. It could be as simple as killing another animal for food which would benefit the hunter, but not the hunted. To live a happy life is to live a life of pleasure and not pain. So the ideal is to minimize pain and violence and living in accordance of excellence. A rough layout would be for all life forms to live in harmony with one another and also in harmony with the environment because the environment plays an important role in our survival. If we ruin the environment in which we live in, such as creating pollution, it could have a negative influence on our health. There is a notion in Buddhism of 'interdependent co-arising', which states that everything is casually dependent upon other things, and that nothing is independent. If we depend on everything else, we must take them into consideration when fulfilling our function.

However, let us be reminded once again that living the good life is much more than merely surviving according to Aristotle because it is possible to live a terrible life filled with pain and violence. We must survive harmoniously with other life forms and with the rest of nature to maximize pleasure and minimize pain. Only then can it be considered the good life, because what is good involves goodness and excellence, not pain, violence, vices, and everything else that is not good. Humans can perform the function extremely well by using our highly developed capacity to reason, and once again, reason is the ultimate human function according to Aristotle.

Human beings, compared to other animals, have a higher level of thinking and reasoning. In Aristotle's version of the functional definition, we would use this rational element to live in conformity with excellence. It would also seem that this rational element among human being provides us with a greater capacity to survive. We dominate this planet because of this capacity to be able to cope and find solutions to many life-threatening problems such as hunger, disease, war, the natural elements, etc. We have a greater chance of survival because we possess the tools and strategies that enable us to control and destroy our enemies. And unlike other animals, we have the capacity to shape our environment. Among the human race, our greatest enemy on this planet would probably be other fellow humans because we posses enough brain power to destroy not only animals, but also each other. Once again, it would seem that we use our reasoning capacity as a means of promoting our survival, which includes living in conformity with excellence. Excellence involves harmony, obtaining the virtues because they are the mean, doing noble and good actions, and happiness. By living in conformity with excellence, we promote our own existence.

On Virtue

Aristotle argues that contemplation aids in human flourishing, but other things are needed as well. He argues that in addition to contemplation, we need to fulfill virtue, which is the means between two extremes. Why should we pursue virtue? The reason for this is because the two extremes (or the vices) will harm us in the end. He first argues that virtue is not innate. We are not born good, or bad, but rather we are socially conditioned to be one way or another. Aristotle argues that if we are born a certain way, then we cannot change it. The example he gives in the *Nicomachean Ethics* is that of the stone. If you roll a stone down a hill, it will always go in one direction. If you through it up in the air, it will fall back down. The stone has a "natural tendency to go downwards," and this is something you cannot change. Virtue, or any sort of moral behavior, is socially conditioned, because if it is not, then we cannot change a person who is naturally evil to be good or vice versa. It is up to our parents, society, and the government to teach us the appropriate behavior.

What are examples of virtue? On the issue of pleasure seeking, too much is called self-indulgence, too little is called being insensible, and the means between two extremes is temperance. On the issue of confidence, too much is called being rash, too little is called being a coward, and the means between the two extremes is called being courageous. Aristotle argues that there is actually not a means to every behavior. Some types of behavior already imply that they are negative. He states:

> [S]ome have names that already imply badness, e.g. spite [feeling of ill will, malice], shamelessness, envy, and in the case of actions adultery, theft, murder; for all of these and suchlike things imply by their names that they are themselves bad, and not the excesses or deficiencies of them" (1107a9 – 11).

Let us explore the first example of the virtue listed above in greater detail. On the issue of pleasure seeking, let us say that it is lunch time and you are extremely hungry. Your body is telling you to go have lunch to fulfill the craving for food, and once you do, you will feel better. In that moment in time, eating food will bring you pleasure because it will get rid of that hunger, which is the displeasure. Let's say you decide to go to McDonald's for lunch, and then you say to the cashier, "I like a Big Mac, a large fries, and a large drink. Also, since I am really hungry, please give me six pieces of chicken nuggets, an apple pie, and an ice-cream Sunday." What will happen if you were to eat all of this food? Even though your hunger will be fulfilled, you ate too much and now you do not feel very good. You have basically self-indulged, which causes a feeling of displeasure to your body. This is an example of one extreme. Let us now say that you are hungry, and you go to McDonald's for lunch, and you say to the cashier, "One water please." What will happen in this scenario? You still feel hungry because you are not fulfilled by just the bottle of water. This would represent the other extreme – being insensible. The means between the two extremes would be ordering just enough food for yourself – not too much, and not too little. Aristotle argues that each individual has to find the appropriate means between two extremes because each person's tolerance is different. We will know when we have reached the extremes when we feel that the activity has undermined our well-being. The vices, therefore, are relative to each individual. Reason also plays in the determination of virtue, which brings us to point of his exact definition in the following passage:

> Virtue, then, is (a) a state that decides, (b) [consisting] in a mean, (c) the mean relative to us, (d) which is defined by reference to reason, (e) i.e., to the reason by reference to which the intelligent person would define it. It is a mean between two vices, one of excess and one of deficiency.

This is another great example of how we use our ability to reason to pursue a more prosperous life, something of which an animal cannot always do, at least not to the extent that we can. In addition to virtue, what is necessary to achieve eudaimonia? Aristotle also argues that we need specific external conditions to prosper in life. Let us now explore what these are.

External Conditions

There are, what are called, external conditions, required to full eudaimonia. These include resources, such as money and power, good health, good family, friends, and even good looks. We need resources such as money simply because the more refined life requires this. Take for example, the issue of education. Being educated at a more prestigious institution will not only develop us into more well-rounded individuals, it will also upon more doors for us in the future. However, being educated at a prestigious institution often correlates with having to obtain a private education, which not only requires an exemplary academic background, extra-curricular background, and leadership background, it also requires a large amount of money. For example, tuition at Stanford University is about $500 per unit. This is the reason why obtaining an elite education in this country is often, but not always, require a privileged background. Aristotle himself came from a rather affluent family, with his father being a medical doctor and having studied under Plato's Academy. Plato himself was from an aristocratic family. Most famous philosophers fall under this camp, which is not surprising. Aristotle also argues that we need good fortune, because even if we have everything else, a stroke of bad fortune can undermine our well-being. This is also not surprising due to the superstitions during ancient Greece.

When Aristotle says that we need good friends, he is referring to virtuous friends, which is the third type of relationship out of four. The first type is relationships based upon utility in which people are used to serve some end goal. The second type is relationships based upon pleasure in which people are used merely for the sake of pleasure. The fourth type is relationships based upon unequals - that is, the status of one is not the same as the other, such as the relationship of a politician and his/her citizens, or parents and their children. The relationship based upon virtue consists of those who pursue eudaimonia, including the virtues. It is a relationship in which both parties can learn and grow from being with each other. A more detailed discussion of Aristotle's four types of relationship can be found within Books VIII and VI of the *Nicomachean Ethics*.

What role do relationships play in eudaimonia? Aristotle argues that we are social animals, and therefore it is natural for us to interact with other people. He also states that it is more enjoyable to engage in activities with other people rather than on our own. For example, on Friday evenings, many people go out and socialize with their friends, such as going to the movies, going out to dinner at Applebee's, going to the bar, etc. It is generally more fun to engage in these activities with other people. People usually do not go out to the movies by themselves, go out to eat by themselves, nor go out to get drunk by themselves. We also need to have a wife or a husband and children. This is where Aristotle's philosophy correlates with the basic function of living organisms, which is not only survival, but to reproduce. It should be noted that Aristotle puts an emphasis on having a *good* family, rather than merely any type of family. Having an undesirable mate or children will, of course, undermine our well being.

On Pursuing Our Talents

Aristotle claims that his philosophy on human flourishing is objective, that is, it can be applied universally to all human beings. Following his philosophy will enable us to achieve the best life possible. His philosophy, however, is not one hundred percent objective. There is a subjective element to his philosophy as well, which lies in the diversity of human talents. A general rule of thumb is that, yes, we should pursue contemplation, a social life, and the external goods that are needed to achieve eudaimonia. However, we do not all have the same talents. This is where Aristotle would argue that whatever talents that we have, we should fulfill these as well. For example, some people are better at leading others, therefore these people should pursue a leadership role in society, such as becoming a manager of a business or becoming a politician. Some people have a talent for art, therefore they should utilize their artistic skills in life. Pursuing such talents will make our life more complete because we "actualize" our potential.

Conclusion

Aristotle's philosophy on eudaimonia, or human flourishing and happiness, requires a multitude of variables. Among these variables includes the pursuit of a contemplative life, and active life, relationships, good family, good friends, good fortune, and resources. We should understand the concept of achieving human potential as laid out by Aristotle and as well as other thinkers, such as the psychologists Abraham Maslow and Carl Jung, in order to understand the concept of eudaimonia. Readers should not mistake Aristotle's philosophy as only emphasizing living the contemplate life because it is the human function, but rather, it is living a holistic life in which we fulfill our human potential. Some of these variables we share with other living organisms such as survival and reproduction, while others are unique to us, primarily our ability to reason, and pursuing talents such as art and music, which are also finer pleasures that cannot be experienced by other animals.

Chapter 3:
Aristotle on Relationships in the *Nicomachean Ethics*, Books VIII and IX

Introduction

Aristotle's argument for the happy person needing virtuous friends in Chapter 9, Book IX of the *Nicomachean Ethics* is divided up into four main parts. The first part is on how "it is more characteristic of a friend to do well by another", in which case we will discuss his notions on why we need friends both in adversity and in prosperity, both of which are actually discussed later in Chapter 11, Book IX of the *Nicomachean Ethics*. The second part is a discussion on how happiness is activity. The third part is on increasing activity by living with friends. The fourth part is a discussion on perception and consciousness as being pleasurable and desirable, in which we will be required to refer back to Chapter 4 of Book IX to Aristotle's discussion on the "man's relationship to himself" in order to better understand his argumentation.

Doing Well by Another

In the first part of Aristotle's argument, he discusses some characteristics of a friend and of the good man, and how "it is more characteristic" for that friend "to do well by another." He states:

> ...It is more characteristic of a friend to do well by another than to be well done by, and to confer benefits is characteristic of the good man and of excellence, and it is nobler to do well by friends than by strangers, the good man will need people to do well by.[4]

The notion of conferring benefits will be better understood if we examine friendship in adversity and in prosperity. To confer benefits on a man in adversity will cheer that man up; it will make that man feel better. This is why we should have friends in adversity. Aristotle states, "...Grief is lightened when friends sorrow with us."[5] That's why we feel better when we have someone to talk to or someone that understands and can feel for our misfortune. He also mentions that the sight of "one's friends is

---

[4] Aristotle, "Nicomachean Ethics", in Jonathan Barnes, ed., *The Complete Works of Aristotle* (Princeton: Princeton U. Press, 1984), 1169^b10-13.

[5] Ibid. 1171^a30.

pleasant" and they become "a safeguard against grief" because they "know our character and the things that please or pain us...."[6] People who are our friends have known us for a certain amount of time and so they know a certain amount about our character, unlike the stranger who does not know anything about us but only have pre-judgments due to stereotypes or other set standards they have for individuals they do not know. Therefore one can be beneficial to a friend in adversity, and to confer benefits is a good and noble thing to do. Not only that, doing so will give a sense of pleasure and happiness, and so it is good to have friends and to confer with them.

In times of prosperity, there are things that we can do to increase our happiness. Aristotle states:

> ...The presence of friends in our prosperity implies both a pleasant passing of our time and the thought of their pleasure at our own good fortune. For this cause it would seem that we ought to summon our friends readily to share our good fortunes (for the beneficent character is a noble one), but summons them to our bad fortunes with hesitation; for we ought to give them as little share as possible in our evils....[7]

Again, we see this notion of a friend benefiting another. In times of prosperity when there is pleasure to be enjoyed, we should share it with other friends so that they could also benefit from our good fortune. It is a good thing to do and we will receive pleasure from doing so. One can argue that not everyone will want to share during times of prosperity. For example, in the case of the man winning the lottery, he may want to keep all his winnings for himself and for his family. Is there an obligation to give a part of his winnings to his friends? If he gives some to his friends, they might want even more because of greed or jealously, especially if the man divides the winnings up unequally among his good friends. If he does not, some of his friends may leave him because they envy him for having so much money and not sharing it. But then again, a friend who feels this way is not the good friend since this sort of friendship is based on utility. So if the man who had won the lottery was a good person and had the best

---

[6] Ibid. 1171^{a}35-1171^{b}5.

[7] Ibid. 1171^{b}13-18.

sort of friendship, one that is based on character and not on utility or pleasure, the good man will share his winnings among his good friends because both parties will benefit from each other. This is partly why Aristotle states that the happy man "will therefore need virtuous friends" because virtuous friends are based on the best form of friendship.[8] What we are describing and what Aristotle is describing are the characteristics of the good friend and the inter-relationship among good friends.

On Solitude

Let us shortly examine Aristotle's discussion on solitude. The purpose for doing so is to bring up an argument against Aristotle's notion on solitude and why men should live among friends. He states:

> ... No one would choose to poses all good things on condition of being alone, since man is a political creature and one whose nature is to live with others. Therefore even the happy man lives with others; for he has the things that are by nature good.[9]

Aristotle believes that we require friends because we are "political creatures" and that a person would not want to "poses all good things" and be alone. What about certain types of people who prefers to live in solitude, for example, monks, nuns, and hermits? They choose to live in solitude, away from society to achieve enlightenment. Buddhists do not even believe in politics. But then again, monks and nuns still live in a community, so there is still the presence of others. What about in the case of the hermit since he or she lives in absolute solitude? One may argue that the goal of monks, nuns, and hermits is not based on happiness and pleasure, or at least Aristotle's version of it. Instead, they are out to achieve liberation through enlightenment; a mental state that surpasses pleasure; a state that involves being one with the universe. But this is an issue for the advanced student or professor of East-Asian philosophies and so it is not appropriate to continue with this discussion any further.

---

[8] Ibid. 1170^b19.

[9] Ibid. $1169^b17\text{-}19$.

Activity and Contemplation are Desirable

The second part of his argument is on activity and contemplation among friends and why they are desirable. Aristotle states:

> If happiness lies in living and being active, and the good man's activity is virtuous and pleasant in itself... and if we can contemplate our neighbours better than ourselves and their actions better than our own, and if the actions of virtuous men who are their friends are pleasant to good men... the blessed man will need friends of this sort....[10]

There are two qualities that a good man has that will benefit us if he is our friend. The first is simply the case that "the good man's activity is virtuous and pleasant in itself" therefore we would want to have friends to perform these activities because they reflect the things that we want for ourselves. The second is that "we can contemplate our neighbors better than ourselves and their actions better than our own."[11] We generally think that we know and understand ourselves better than anyone does, but sometimes it takes another a friend to understand our character and our actions because they have a separate mind aside from ours, and so they are able to contemplate us from a different perspective. For example, when we do things unconsciously, we are not able to explain the reasoning behind these acts, but a friend might be able to because he knows from experience that we do certain things for certain reasons. That is why a mother, because she knows her child since birth, will understand the child's wants and needs better than her own child could. For this reason, we should have friends because we benefit from their contemplation about us, therefore allowing us to know ourselves better from a non-subjective point of view. In this segment, Aristotle concludes:

> ...The blessed man will need friends of this sort, since he chooses to contemplate worthy actions and actions that are his own, and the actions of a good man who is his friend have both these qualities.[12]

---

[10] Ibid. 1169^b31-1170^a2.

[11] Ibid. 1169^b33-34.

[12] Ibid. 1170^a2-3.

Living Among Others Increases Activity

The third part of Aristotle's argument is on increasing activity by living with friends. If happiness is an activity, it would make sense for us to increase our activity in order to increase our happiness. He states:

> Further, men think that the happy man ought to live pleasantly. Now if he were a solitary, life would be hard for him; for by oneself it is not easy to be continuously active, but with others it is easier.[13]

By living among friends, one can perform a variety of activities with them. Aristotle mentions a couple of these activities in Chapter 12, Book IX that includes drinking together, exercising, hunting, and studying philosophy together.[14] Each "class of men" will do the things that they love most.[15] There are certain things that a person would prefer to do with friends and not by one self, for example, going out to eat, attending a concert, or going to the theatre, for these activities are more enjoyable when done with friends, partly because we merely enjoy the presence of our friends. And there are other activities that do require more than one person to fulfill like competing in sporting events or playing chess (with the exception of playing against a computer).

If we do not enjoy the presence of our friends or if the activity does not require other people to perform, would it be acceptable, then, to perform these activities on our own? For example, one can read philosophy by oneself because this sort of activity does not require friends. But then another may argue against this because when one contemplates about philosophy, it is more interesting and pleasurable to do so among a group of friends because the act of contemplation increases when there are other people contemplating also. What about people who meditates such as monks and nuns? Meditation is an individual activity that requires silence and concentration. Therefore it would be best to have the least number of people around during the meditative process. Meditating alone would probably be the ideal. What about in the case of the introverted versus the

---

[13] Ibid. 1170^a4-6.

[14] Ibid. 1172^a3-5.

[15] Ibid. 1172^a5.

extroverted person? Introverted people are more individualistic and less sociable than extroverted people. Would Aristotle, then, consider extroverted people better than introverted people since extraverted people are more sociable and perform more activities with others, even though the introverted person is happy the way he or she is?

According to Aristotle, the more we perform activities among good friends, the better we will become as a good person because the actions of good people are good in themselves. The actions of good and virtuous people are regarded as pleasurable in themselves, and they are things that the good person wants for one self. This is probably why Aristotle states, "A certain training in excellence arises also from the company of the good...."[16] The friendship of good people is good because of its beneficial characteristics and the friendship of bad people is the opposite. Aristotle sums it up in the following statement:

> Thus the friendship of bad men turns out an evil thing (for because of their instability they united in bad pursuits, and besides they become evil by becoming like each other), while the friendship of good men is good, being augmented by their companionship; and they are thought to become better too by their activities and by improving each other; for from each other they take the mould of the characteristics they approve....[17]

One may argue that even among bad men, there are certain characteristics seen as pleasurable and desirable, and they also become better at the activities that they do. A group of auto thieves become better at hi-jacking cars over time. In other words, they become better at the activity, but will they become better as individuals? Aristotle would not agree because the nature of the activity is bad in itself. Auto thieves are thieves, and so their character is made up of things such as dishonestly, lying, and cheating – all of which are not the characteristics of the good or virtuous person.

---

[16] Ibid. 1170^{a}11-12.

[17] Ibid. 1127^{a}7-14.

Perception is Pleasurable and Desirable

The fourth part in Aristotle's argument on why the happy man needs virtuous friends is based on perception and why it's pleasurable and desirable. Aristotle states:

> Perceiving that one lives is one of the things that are pleasant in themselves (for life is by nature good, and to perceive what is good present in oneself is pleasant)... Life is desirable, and particularly so for the good men, because to them existence is good and pleasant (for they are pleased at the consciousness of what is in itself good)....[18]

According to Aristotle, "life is by nature good" and the act of perceiving and being conscious is pleasurable. If it is pleasurable, then the good man will desire it. Since consciousness of one's goodness is pleasurable and desirable, the perception of a friend is also pleasurable because a friend is like another self.[19] Friends help make us more conscious of ourselves, which is also desirable. In order to understand why a friend is like another self, we would have to refer back to Chapter 4 of Book IX on the discussion of "the man's relationship to himself". Aristotle believes that the man "wishes for himself what is good" and "does so for his own sake" for these are "characteristics of the good man."[20] Therefore, it is natural to desire friends who have the same attributes since these are the characteristics of the good man as we have discussed earlier. Since the consciousness of our own existence is desirable, so would the existence of a friend, and for this reason one should live among friends and contemplate with each other.[21]

---

[18] Ibid. $1170^b 1$-5.

[19] Ibid. $1170^b 5$-7.

[20] Ibid. $1166^a 13$-18.

[21] Ibid. $1170^b 10$-13.

Conclusion

We have discussed the reasons why Aristotle believes that the happy man needs virtuous friends. The first reason is because one can benefit from the act of conferring, and examples were giving in times of adversity and in times of prosperity. The second reason is that happiness is an activity, and the actions of virtuous friends are good, and what is good is pleasurable, and what is pleasurable is desirable. The third reason for having friends is because one can increase the amount of activity by living among friends since many activities are done with friends and not by one self. The fourth reason is that perception and consciousness are desirable, including that of our own existence and that of friends because friends are like another self and they help make us more conscious of ourselves. We desire the good characteristics within us and so we desire them among friends also. These are the four main reasons why Aristotle argues that the happy man needs virtuous friends.

Chapter 4:
The Search for Guiding Principles in Natural Law Theory

Introduction

The foundation of social and political governance can be found through the investigation of natural law theory. This investigation will help us to extrapolate fundamental guiding principles that can be used as the end goals at which we are aiming for, and based on these end goals, we can then engineer a social, economic, and political system that will enable us to achieve these goals.

There are several and distinct versions of natural law, which can be categorized as being either secular or non-secular. The secular version is derived from pure reason and observation of the natural world, and this takes on two forms as well: 1) There are universal principles out there that can guide human behavior, and 2) The contemporary deontological version, in which "humanitarian norms are discernible through reason, and the legitimacy of the legal order comes from the ethics of rights reason."[22] In general, natural law theorists derive normative statements from descriptive ones. For example, from the descriptive statement that living organisms have a tendency to strive toward self-preservation, I can posit the claim that self-preservation is a natural right. From this, I can come up with a normative principle such as, "Every individual has a right to practice self-preservation, and no other person may interfere with this right." The non-secular version states that natural law is derived from God's law, and is therefore contingent in the faith that God exist.

Natural law theorists will posit fundamental principles that aim at certain end goals. An example would John Finnis' principle of human flourishing. I argue that there are very few end goals that are deemed universal. This is due to different beliefs held by people within different cultures, across different periods of history. People from different cultures will have a different reasoning process, and so they interpret things in the context of their culture. In this chapter, I will discuss the basic conception of natural law and its criticisms. I will also discuss a non-secular version of natural law, the classical Thomist tradition, and then I will discuss the secular version of natural law. It will become apparent to the reader that

---

[22] Robert L. Hayman, Jr., Nancy Levit, and Richard Delgado, eds. *Jurisprudence Classical and Contemporary: From Natural Law to Postmodernism* (St. Paul, MN: West Group, 2002) 2.

the fundamental principles and end goals vary from one version of natural law to the next.

Basic Conception of Natural Law

Some basic underlying premises of natural law are: 1.) Human nature is universal, 2.) There are inherent purposes or self-evident goods for living organisms, 3.) These goods are discovered through reason and observation of the natural world, 4.) Morality is universal, objective, and are also discovered through reason, and 5.) Human laws must reflect natural laws.

S.B. Dury provides a more detailed discussion of the relationship between human law and natural law.[23] Dury mentions one core idea that underlies natural law is the implication that there is a universal justice "that transcends the particular expressions of justice in any given set of positive laws," and that these "universal principles of justice are accessible to reason and independent of human volition."[24] Furthermore, any positive laws contrary to these are not really law since they lack "the moral content necessary to put us under obligation."[25] Natural law philosophers will also argue that valid law is binding not only because authority enforces it, but also because it has intrinsic worth. Dury also makes the distinction between a valid law and a viable law. "A morally iniquitous [or unjust] law cannot be *valid*."[26] A valid law must have moral content, or conform to natural law. "This is a law that is worthy of obedience and capable of obligating the rational intelligence."[27] The law is *viable* when it produces the desired effect – "eliciting the voluntary compliance of those it protects in order to coerce the rest."[28] Another distinction between valid law and

---

[23] S.B. Dury, "H.L.A. Hart's Minimum Content Theory of Natural Law", *Political Theory* 9(4) (November, 1981) 533 – 546.

[24] Ibid. 534.

[25] Ibid.

[26] Ibid.

[27] Ibid. 542.

[28] Ibid.

viable law is that the latter is determined by the status quo, while the former is not. A valid law is therefore valid solely because it has moral content, and not because a majority of people agrees that it should be valid. These objective moral principles are discovered through reason, and not through the appeal of the masses.

When there is a discussion of natural law, it is often associated with natural rights. What is the distinction between the two? Natural law tends to describe a normative social order, while natural rights describe the rights of individuals. Natural law is dependent on natural rights, since the former is to protect the latter in a social community. One can argue that natural laws and natural rights can be established without a civil government. Any individual with the proper intellect can derive these from reason and experience of the natural world.

An important distinction to make in natural law theory (since it has led to some confusion) is between descriptive statements and prescriptive statements. The former describes the nature of reality, while the latter are normative statements, which states that human beings should do certain things for certain reasons. But how are we able to derive normative statements from descriptive ones about the world? What is the connection? S.B. Dury provided a good discussion to show the relationship between dynamic law (which is a descriptive law) and moral law. Dury states that there are two kinds of empirical laws: the mechanical and the dynamic. The former are strict and unalterable, such as the laws of gravity or thermodynamics. Dynamic laws reflect the biological world and its dynamic or changing behavior. The fact that biological life grows, develops, and dies suggests that dynamic laws are not static like mechanical laws. Both internal factors, such as my mental state, and external factors, such as the environment that I live in, will have an affect on biological life. "[T]he development of growing things is contingent on the existence of favorable conditions" and "[a]ltering these conditions will invariably impede or enhance the development of the thing in question."[29] This is where the relationship between descriptive laws and prescriptive laws come in:

---

[29] Dury, 537.

> The dynamic laws of nature can be said to be related to moral laws in two ways. First, it is good that living things reach their optimum condition unimpeded. Second, potentiality sets limits to achievement. Thus, the good for man must depend on what man *can* achieve in view of his given potentialities. In other words, Ought must imply *Can*, even though what man can do and what he ought to do are not identical.[30]

Dury made an important connection here, especially about the part that ought must imply can, since there's no purpose in saying that a person should behave in a way if it is not achievable. Furthermore, it makes sense to say that if there is a way (e.g., a certain lifestyle) for me to achieve an optimum condition unimpeded, I should follow this path only if I want to. Just because there is an optimal way of living and that it is highly valued to live this way does not mean that I am obligated to do so. No one can force this upon me. It is up to me whether or not I want to live a superior life. The choices that we make are partly determined by our values and our end goals, and these are strongly influenced by the culture that we live in. For this reason, cultural relativists will argue that there is no universal human nature or moral principles. I will explore this and other criticisms of natural law theory later in this paper.

The Non-secular Version of Natural Law

Natural law can be approached from two perspectives: the secular and the non-secular. The former is often associated with rationalism, and the latter with God's laws. On the other hand, St. Thomas Aquinas in the classical tradition of natural law (also known as the Thomist tradition) combines rationalism with the divine. Let us now explore the non-secular version of natural law.

The non-secular version of natural law is dependent on the ontology, or existence, of God. Those who believe in this view have the burden of proving God's existence and how they came to know that these laws are God's genuine laws. Since this version of natural law is dependent on God's existence, not being able to prove His existence would undermine the theory. The only other way I can see the theory hold is if God really did exist, but we cannot be certain of this. Since the different arguments

---

[30] Ibid.

for the existence of God (e.g., the teleological argument, the ontological argument, the first cause argument) are all weak, there doesn't seem to be anything left except a reliance upon faith. Nevertheless, let us explore some of the criticisms of the classical theory of natural law, also known as the Thomist tradition.

St. Thomas Aquinas combined rationalism and the divine in his theory of natural law, so it has the best of both worlds. H.L.A. Hart describes the Thomist tradition of natural law as follows:

> The Thomist tradition of Natural Law comprises a twofold contention: first, that there are certain principles of true morality or justice, discoverable by human reason without the aid of revelation even though they have a divine origin; secondly, that man-made laws which conflict with these principles are not valid law.[31]

In addition to the mechanical principles of this world, there are universal human principles (e.g., morality and justice) that can also be discovered through reason. Hart states that we do not have to rely on the revelation of God in order to derive these principles. For instance, it would be accurate to describe living organisms as having a basic tendency to strive towards self-preservation. The best condition to achieve this is an unimpeded one. If a person wants to achieve this, it is his or her right to do so. It would be wrong for someone else to interfere with this process. Other normative principles can be derived from this principle, such as, 1) one should treat others the way you want to be treated, 2) one should not harm another person's life, and 3) one should take proper care of one's mind and body. These normative principles help us to insure growth, development, and survival, which are some of the end goals in life. In these examples, one does not need the revelation of God, but only an appeal to the basic human tendencies. This would also mean that the secular theorists can also come up with these exact same normative principles and end goals of human nature without relying on the existence of God. In science, this would be known as a simpler theory, and therefore better.

---

[31] H.L.A. Hart, *The Concept of Law* (Oxford: Oxford University Press, 1961) 152.

Hart argues that natural law has not always been associated with the divine. It has its "roots in Greek thought which was, for this purpose, quite secular."[32] He also makes the claim that at least some form of natural law is independent of both divine authority and human authority, which is exactly why it is considered a law of nature. Furthermore, if natural laws are to hold universally, they cannot be dependent upon any particular religion because each religion does not have the exact same doctrine and beliefs as another's. For the same reason, natural law cannot be dependent upon any particular group of people, society, or culture. Let us now explore an alternative version of natural law.

The Secular Version of Natural Law

One version in the rationalist tradition is the view that natural laws are derived from existing universal principles. These laws are derived from observation, just like the laws of physics or thermodynamics. Since they are there to begin with, we do not create them, but rather we discover them. In this secular view, "nature is the scene of recurrent changes revealing distinct regularities."[33] These distinct regularities explain how nature operates and it allows us to predict what will occur. If I throw a rock off of a cliff, it will fall down to the bottom due to the law of gravity. This must always be true unless the Earth's gravitational pull is somehow altered, causing the rock not to fall to the bottom. If at some point the law fails to explain the event, my construction and explanation of the law is flawed, not the actual law itself, and I must alter it accordingly to reflect the actual law. We can see this happening when there is a paradigm shift in science. For example, at one point in history, many people thought that the Earth was the center of the Universe. Another example is that at one point in history, many people thought that the world was flat. One of the limitations of deriving the laws of nature, such as physical laws, is the limit of our technology, mathematical theory, physical theory, and the like. How these observational events occur is how they ought or should occur; if I throw a rock off of a cliff, it ought to fall to the bottom due to the law of gravity. In this version of natural law, I would observe human behavior

---

[32] Ibid. 183.

[33] Dury, 535.

and conclude that humans have a tendency to strive toward certain end goals, such as the tendency to live, to grow and evolve, to pursue pleasure, and to avoid pain. Then I can come up with normative principles to guide me toward these goals. This is the basic structure of natural law. It is a natural law because the descriptive statements about human nature are true, and it is a moral system because it contains normative statements.

The other secular version of natural law theory is the teleological version. Not only are regularities predictable, everything has a tendency to move towards a certain direction:

> In contrast to the secular view of nature, the teleological view does not simply reflect regularities that are predictable; instead, everything in nature is seen as tending toward a definite optimum state that constitutes the specific good, end, or *telos* appropriate for it. The telos of a thing describes the optimum state of its development of maturity. The man also has a telos or optimum state which is given, not just arbitrarily chosen by him. Man may desire his good or end, but it is not his good merely because he *desires* it. On the contrary, he desires it because it is already his natural end.[34]

Aristotle writes that the *telos* (function or chief end) of humankind is to achieve eudemonia, or happiness in the fullest sense. Eudemonia is an activity of the soul, and this is regarded as being the ultimate end goal. "Human good turns out to be activity of soul in conformity with excellence, and if there are more than one excellence, in conformity with the best and most complete."[35] Excellence can be spoken of in two ways: 1) intellectual excellence, which includes philosophic wisdom, practical wisdom, and understanding, and 2) moral excellence, which involves liberality and temperance. Moral excellence is primarily the practice of achieving the mean between two vices, and this is how we achieve temperance. For example, the mean between fear and confidence is courage, the mean between giving too much money and taking too much

---

[34] Ibid. 535.

[35] Aristotle, "Nicomachean Ethics," trans. W.D. Ross, *The Complete Works of Aristotle*, ed. Jonathan Barnes, vol. 2 (Princeton, NJ: Princeton UP, 1995) 1098a15.

money is liberality, the mean between honor and dishonor is proper pride, and the mean between irascible and irascibility is good temper. The practice of moral excellence is the normative claim; we ought to strive for the mean between two vices because the vices will eventually undermine us. Doing this will help us to achieve eudemonia.

Some, including H.L.A. Hart will say that the only end is human survival. S.B. Dury has argued against this position. Mere survival is not the human telos for two reasons:

> First, it does not reflect an optimum condition of fulfillment. Second, the telos of man is not dependent on human volition. The proper end of man is independent of whether or not an overwhelming majority happen to desire it. Unlike survival, it is not contingent on the fact that 'most men most of the time wish to continue in existence'.[36]

The classical notion of telos is achieving "the most complete fulfillment of human potentialities."[37] Survival does not fulfill this role. The tendency to promote self-preservation is not unique to humans, but an elementary tendency found in all living organisms. Dury also suggests that being a moral agent is an important part of understanding the human telos. A person can perform both moral and immoral acts in order to stay alive. Since survival does not always promote morals, it alone cannot be the telos of man. Furthermore, survival is contingent upon one's desire, and the classical notion of the end of man cannot be contingent. Certainly there are people who do not wish to live any longer for whatever reason (e.g., depression, terminal illness, etc.), but whether or not these people want to live is a separate question from what is the proper end and function of humankind. The proper end is good in itself regardless of human volition (whether people fulfill it or not), and it does not rely upon the approval of the majority. If it did rely on any individual, this end would be relative and not objective. The classical notion of human telos posits the claim that fulfilling our potential is good and is an end in itself, and from this, they posit the normative claim that we ought to strive towards achieving our full human potential.

---

[36] Dury, 538.

[37] Ibid. 538 -539.

S.B. Dury also argues against Hart's position that this teleological view applies both to the inanimate things as well as animates things. According to Dury, it only makes sense for us to apply the notion of teleology to the biological world through its dynamic nature. It would not make sense to apply it to the inanimate, solely mechanical world. A rock at the bottom of the hill is no more or less in an optimum state than at the top of the hill. On the other hand, the dynamic laws of the biological world, as was discussed earlier, have a relationship with moral laws – that it is good to achieve the optimum state unimpeded. If I want to achieve the optimum state and make this my end goal, I should take the route that contains the least amount of constraint. We must remember that this is a descriptive claim about living organisms – that it is natural for them to develop and to grow, and it is good to do so unimpeded. A normative claim can be derived from this descriptive claim about achieving the optimum state, such as, "A person ought to be allowed to develop, grow, and live an unimpeded life." In this instance, the development of biological organisms becomes an inherent right. Of course, the government and the law may interfere with this right if this person undermines the development, growth, and livelihood of another person. It is the duty of the commonwealth to protect this and other human rights.

The biological tendency towards development and growth can be categorized under life, which is one of the fundamental values or basic human goods according to John Finnis. His system of natural law is more complex because it has two tiers. The first constitutes human flourishing. There are seven forms of human good at this level: 1) life, which includes bodily health, reproduction, and of course the freedom from pain, 2) knowledge, 3) play, 4) aesthetic experience, 5) sociability, 6) practical reasonableness, which is "the capacity to impose an intelligent and reasonable order upon deliberation about the pursuit of basic goods," and 7) religion.[38] These basic goods are regarded as being inherently good, and they are end in themselves. They are the pre-moral standards of natural law, but they appear to be limited in scope. It is possible to derive a more refined version of these human goods, such as one that would include

---

[38] Charles Covell, "The Defense of Natural Law Theory" (New York: St. Martin's Press, 1992) 200.

pleasure as being a fundamental good. Pleasure would encapsulate aesthetic experience along with other forms of pleasure.

The second tier consists of normative principles, or methodological requirements, for practical deliberation. These normative principles help guide the person in the pursuit of the seven basic human goods, and it enables the person to distinguish between what is morally right and morally wrong. The requirements are to:

> ...form and pursue a coherent life plan with consistent principles, have no arbitrary preferences among values or persons, respect every basic value in every act, promote the common good, treat others as one would wish to be treated, be committed to a life plan but sufficiently detached for objectivity, follow one's conscience, and avoid consequentialism or utilitarianism.[39]

These are the things that we ought to do according to Finnis, but only if we agree that the seven basic goods are inherent in themselves, and if we deem them worthy of pursuit. He also makes the claim that these human goods can only be secured through human laws. This is the purpose of the judicial institution, and this is why we need a sovereign power, which is similar to Locke's notion of having a commonwealth to protect our natural rights.

Kent Greenawalt criticizes Finnis for being too abstract and categorical.[40] The basic human values, including life, are incommensurable (not measurable like the principle of utility). According to Finnis, we should never act against these basic values. For instance, if I had to the choice to kill one innocent person in order to save 1,000 other people, it would be wrong to kill this person because it would undermine the basic principle of life. Furthermore, killing this person would be using him as a means to an end, and this according to Finnis, is not permissible. But not doing so would undermine the lives of 1,000 people. What if this one person chooses to sacrifice his or her life in order to save others? Would it

---

[39] John Finnis, "Natural Law and Natural Rights," in *Jurisprudence Classical and Contemporary: From Natural Law to Postmodernism*, R.L Hayman, Jr., N. Leviit, and R. Delgado, eds. (St. Paul, MN: West Group, 2002) note 1, pg. 28.

[40] See Kent Greenawalt, "How Persuasive is Natural Law Theory?", *Notre Dame Law Review* 75 (August, 2000) 1647 – 1679.

then be okay to kill this person? Greenawalt acknowledges the difficulties when there is a conflict between the basic values, and he suggests that aesthetic experience should not be valued over life. He gives us an example of when we should prefer one good over the other. In his example, ten foreign visitors are allowed into a small museum on a day that it is closed. The manager was nice enough to let them in because they have to fly back to Asia that same evening. A man becomes outraged because of this. He pulls out a gun and threatens to shoot the museum guard unless they force the ten foreign visitors to leave. In this instance, Greenawalt argues that saving the museum guard would be the morally responsible thing to do. In order to do this, the manager of the museum must deny the ten foreign visitors an aesthetic experience. Under this and under similar circumstances, it would be appropriate to choose one good over the other. For this reason, Finnis' absolutist approach is regarded as being too rigid, and that it should be flexible enough to deal with different situations in different cultures. People often make moral decisions based on several factors, including the legality of a country's law and its cultural values and norms. Some people are more lenient and treat people more kindly and with more respect than others, which leads them to act differently than those who are not as kind and as respectful.

Criticisms of Natural Law Theory

Greenawalt also cites some of the traditional criticisms of natural law early in his essay, including historicism, cultural relativism, and the argument from anthropology. The basic argument from these three perspectives is that "there is no universal human nature, no transcultural reason, [and] no objective moral perspective."[41] Anthropologists argue that much of human characteristics are culture dependent. "The same is true about human reason; to a substantial degree our sense of what is reasonable depends on our culture and our particular place within it."[42] Nevertheless, there are some things that all of us share such as, the desire for food, well-being, and companionship. The difference in our mode of

---

[41] Ibid. 1658.

[42] Ibid.

thinking leads us to have a slightly or drastically different understanding of these goods. Furthermore, we rate each good differently from each other. For example, in a communal society such as that of the Native Americans, much of their property was held collectively, and more emphasis was given to the group rather than the individual. The collective good was more important than individual good. In our current society, we value personal property more than communal property. There is a greater emphasis on individual autonomy, and less on the collective. If property were held as being a fundamental good that increases human flourishing, it would rank differently between these two cultures. It would be ranked higher (as being more valuable) in our culture than in the Native American culture because we value having private property more than sharing it with other people.

Greenawalt suggests that the radical form of this criticism will deny that moral questions have correct answers. A less radical version will doubt that "these answers will reach across cultures and that they can be discovered by cross-cultural reason."[43] Both versions undermine the premises underlying natural law theory. He goes on to say that "the real issue about universality is not either/or, but more or less."[44] This is not a correct statement because a universal theory would have to apply to every single culture. It should not be culture dependent, nor is it historically dependent. Something is either universal, or it is not. It is appropriate to say that some moral principles apply more broadly across a variety of cultures than others. In such instances, it would not be appropriate to use the term 'universal' or 'universality' because for it to apply broadly does not entail universality. Universal entails "in all instances". This is why I argue that natural law theory has very few principles and end goals that can be truly said to be universal, and most of these are descriptive statements about the basic and natural tendencies of living organism, such as self-preservation, growth, development, and well-being.

---

[43] Ibid.

[44] Ibid.

Conclusion

The classical version of natural law faced many criticisms because of its claim that natural law has a divine origin. Nevertheless, it still contains many principles, including Aquinas's principles of virtue that are useful because they help lead us to the proper human telos. But even this is interpreted differently by different theorists. Aristotle would say that the goal is to achieve eudemonia by acting in accordance with excellence. For John Finnis, it is to promote human flourishing, or the seven basic human goods, and the methodological requirements allow us to pursue these. A biologist would say that the function of all life is to develop, grow, stay alive, and procreate, and do so with the least amount of inhibiting factors. What we ought to do are the things that would help us achieve these end goals. If we come to a rational decision that these end goals are truly good for us, then we should follow normative principles given by each respective natural law theory in order to achieve the end goal. If we make the rational decision that there doesn't seem to be any purpose or obligation to follow these principles. But rationality isn't the only factor when it comes to making these types of decisions. A lot of it has to do with having the proper motivation and the resources to pursue these ends. For instance, a homeless person will have a difficult time perusing even the basic goals in life, such as getting enough food to stay alive.

Different versions of natural law theory contain slightly different principles to achieve the end goals. We have seen that there is lack of universal agreement on what the end goals of humanity are, except for self-preservation, growth, development, and well-being. Many political theorists such as Hobbes and Locke proposed that it is the role of the commonwealth to uphold certain normative principles in order for each person to achieve these end goals in life. Different versions of natural law theory contain a hint of personal and cultural subjectivity, which undermines the very essence of what natural law theory is supposed to be. Natural law theory is supposed to be purely objective and universal, not subjective and culture dependent.

Chapter 5:
Mill and Kant on Morality

Introduction

What is the right thing to do? Is morality objective or subjective? Should we act out of reason to avoid biasness or should we out of inclination because we are naturally biased and emotional beings? Every person operates upon some ethical foundation. Our ethical values come from a variety of sources. Some of which are from our parents, some are from society, some are from the people we spend time with such as our friends, and some are even derived internally by our emotions and personal biasness. This chapter will explore two classical ethical theories. One is called utilitarianism by Jeremy Bentham, which was later adopted by his son, John Stuart Mill. The other is the categorical imperative by Immanuel Kant. Utilitarianism is a consequentialist theory; what is right and wrong is contingent upon the end result or the consequence of the action. This is contrary to Kant's theory because the categorical imperative is a formalist theory. What is right and wrong for Kant has nothing to do with the end results. Some things are good in themselves, while others are not. This is based upon Kant's utopia called the Kingdom of Ends in which everyone is a moral judge and a moral legislature. Both theories have strengths and weaknesses. Most of us will find that we incorporate both Mill's theory and Kant's theory into our daily lives even though we might not know of their theories beforehand. Let us first explore Mill's theory.

Utilitarianism

The British philosophy Jeremy Bentham developed the theory of utilitarianism, which was later adopted by his son, John Stuart Mill. The theory of utilitarianisms states that the right thing to do is "to maximize happiness for the greatest number of people while taking into consideration everyone involved." In any given situation, therefore, the right thing to do is to act in such a way to maximize happiness in the end. For example, let us say that there is a water raft, and there are ten people stuck on this water raft in the middle of the ocean. There are only enough food rations for seven people, and that three people will likely die of starvation. Help is coming soon, but they will have to manage on their own until it does. The right thing to do in this case would be to give the food rations to the seven people on the raft that would give back to society the most based upon their occupation, skill, knowledge, and talents. Sacrificing three people is justified to achieve a greater good. This is why this theory is considered a consequentialist theory because the right thing to do is contingent on the end result.

What criticisms can be raised against utilitarianism? The first is the problem of calculation. It is not always possible to accurately measure happiness, pleasure, or "positive hedons" to determine the end result. The second problem is the problem of rights and the problem of justice. One can argue that the three people on the water raft that didn't receive rations because they are determined as being "the least valuable" to society is unfair and unjust. They have a right to life like any other human beings and it would be immoral to sacrifice them solely based upon their contributions to society. There are also times when we should act out of duty rather than to maximize happiness. For instance, imagine that there is a burning house, and inside the house is a priest and your uncle. The priest is doing a lot for society and your uncle is just an average person with an average job. You respect and love your uncle very much because he is a very nice person and he is a blood relative. The priest is a complete stranger. Who would you save in this instance? Many people would say that they would save their uncle simply because there is a duty to our family members first and foremost, even though the priest will contribute more to this world than your uncle. In times like this, people will usually not prefer to act according to utilitarianism.

The Categorical Imperative

The German philosopher Immanuel Kant felt that acting out of inclination (personal biasness or emotions), like in the above example, is problematic. He argued that morality should be universal, objective, and rational. Certain things are always right and certain things are always wrong. His moral theory is called the categorical imperative and it consists of two formulations.

The first formulation of the categorical imperative is "to act in such a way that your maxim can be made into a universal law." What this means is that we should act in such a way that your action can be made into a universal law where everyone is willing to act on it as well. Let us use lying as an example. All we have to do is to plug lying into the formula and determine whether it will fulfill the rule. Can lying be universalized? What would happen if we were to live in a world where it is okay to lie and everyone, or at least the majority, lies? If you go to the bank and ask for a loan, you will be turned down because the bank knows that people break their promise to return the money. If a friend asks you that he or she needs money for lunch and would like to borrow five dollars from you, you will not give your friend the money. Once again, in a world where lying is universal, you know that your friend will not pay you back. For this reason, lying is morally wrong according to Kant.

The second formulation is "to never use people as a means to an end." Kant expects us to treat everyone with respect; people are inherently valuable. In order to understand this concept, we need to understand his philosophy of the "Kingdom of Ends" in which everyone is a moral judge and a moral legislature. In this utopia, everyone treats everyone else equally. Whatever I do will not only benefit me, it will benefit everyone else. No one is harmed or used in the process and everyone is treated fairly. To use people or to undermine people in any way implies that I am somehow better than the person I am using or undermining, and for Kant, this is morally unjustifiable. In the example of the water raft, Kant would say that it is morally wrong to sacrifice three people for the greater good. To do so is to use them to benefit the greater good, and that they are dispensable because they are inferior. Every human life is as valuable as every other human life. It is also for this reason that killing innocent people is always considered wrong.

Kant distinguishes between perfect duties and imperfect duties. Perfect duties are actions that must always be upheld. Among these are not killing innocent people, not lying, and not breaking a promise. It is never permissible for us to undermine our perfect duties. There are also imperfect duties, and these are actions that we do not always have to fulfill. These include developing one's talents and helping the needy.

There are also several criticisms to Kant's categorical imperative. The first is that it is unlikely possible to never use in life. We use other people on a constant basis. When we go to the store, we are using the cashier to ring up our purchases. The cashier is there using the business, and the business is using the customers to make money. When we are children, we use our parents because we need them to provide us with the basic necessities. In relationships, people use each other for love, attention, pleasure, and happiness. To use people, then, is not necessary a bad thing. One can also say that it is unlikely to never lie in life as well. There might be times when it is necessary and even appropriate to lie, for instance, to avoid hurting a person's feelings. Also, we might have to lie to save a person's life. Under these circumstances, many would agree that lying is permissible. These criticisms show us that Kant's theory is too rigid. We do not live in the ideal world where everyone is a moral judge and a moral legislature. Furthermore, people do not always act out of pure reason. Our behaviors also involve personal biasness and emotions (like in the example of saving our uncle over the priest inside the burning house). Furthermore, due to Kant's religious background, he believed that the Earth was create for us, therefore, everyone on it, including animals, are here for us to use. It is okay for us to use animals, but it is not okay for us to use other human beings. His religious devotion also led him to say that suicide and all forms of euthanasia are wrong because God originally created life, and life is inherently valuable. Some may argue that under extreme pain, suicide or euthanasia is justifiable, for example, in the case of a terminally ill person dying of cancer. Kant's theory, therefore, is too rigid.

Conclusion

The principle of utilitarianism states that the right thing to do is to maximize happiness for the greatest number of people, taking into account everyone. It is justifiable for us to sacrifice some people to save others in order to contribute to the greater good. It is justifiable to not fulfill our duty of choosing our relative over a stranger if the stranger will contribute more to this world than our relative. The categorical imperative consists of two formulations. The first is to act in such a way that our maxim can be made into a universal law. The second is to never use people as a means to an end. Kant also believed that killing innocent people, lying, and breaking a promise is never permissible. However, it is unlikely that we can go through life without ever using people, lying to people, or break a promise. We are not purely rational beings. We often act out of personal biasness and emotions. Neither moral theory is perfect. People do not always have to prefer one over the other. There are some instances where we may feel that maximizing happiness is the right thing to do. Other times, we may feel that it is right to fulfill our perfect duties according to Kant.

Chapter 6:
Machiavelli on the Ethics of Political Power

Introduction

One central theme in Machiavelli's writings is the use of evil to achieve a certain end. In the *Prince*, evil is necessary for the prince to maintain power. In the *Discourses*, evil is justified to help establish and maintain a republic. I will argue against Machiavelli's thesis that non-virtuous actions are justified when they help the prince to maintain his power or when it is required to maintain order in the republic. When evil methods are used, individual rights such as liberty, autonomy, justice, and equality are violated. But since each government must limit the rights of its citizens to maintain the stability of society as a whole, it would be impossible for them to not use any sort of evil or non-virtuous methods at all, especially when fighting an internal or an external war. Therefore, the real question should be, "To what extent is the use of non-virtuous behavior justified?" The approach that will promote long-term stability of the state should be preferred over what does not. I do not believe Machiavelli's approach will achieve this. In this chapter, I will examine Machiavelli's argument for the use of cruelty and wickedness. I will also apply his theory to the American Empire by examining the justification of its evil acts, both domestic and abroad, including the recent invasion and occupation of Iraq.[45] We will quickly realize that an abuse of power and violence in the short-term will likely to cause destabilization in the long-term.

On Justice

Justice (in the ordinary sense) is not a part of Machiavelli's use of virtue. His notion of virtue is related to war – having courage, patience, strength, being skillful, etc. In a memorandum of 1506 and in *La caginoe dell' ordinanza*, he mentions that government requires "justice and arms" to keep the subjects in order and to protect against foreign attack. His notion of justice is a form of political order. This is referred to as being

---

[45] U.S. government officials did not want to call the presence of U.S. soldiers in Iraq as being an "occupation" even though foreign news services did. Corporate owned domestic news services (e.g., CNN) eventually gave in and began using the word occupation along with the civilized countries (e.g., Canada, France, and Germany).

positive justice – "justice consequent on the establishment of laws on the basis of power."[46] This helps us to understand why Machiavelli justifies certain non-virtuous activities to maintain order in the republic. Let us now examine specific passages in which Machiavelli talks about the methods used to establish political order.

Justification of Evil Acts in the *Prince*

If one only reads the *Prince* and takes it at face value, it would seem as though Machiavelli is in favor of tyrannical rule. The *Prince* is a manual for a prince to come into power, maintain that power, and maintain control over the people. Ways for the prince to retain power is to eliminate any threats by killing off opponents, and basically doing whatever else it takes in order to maintain power even if it involves what seem to be immoral acts. Of course, Machiavelli only wrote the *Prince* to please the Medici family (the family that ruled Florence), hoping that they will employ him in their government even though he was captured and tortured by the same authorities for plotting against the government. It is not until one reads the *Discourses* that the reader will realize Machiavelli is trying to promote a republic, not a tyrannical principality. However, he does keep a lot of the same ideas in the *Discourses* as he does in the *Prince* when it comes to establishing law and order, or justice, in the society. This will become apparent when we examine some of the passages from the *Discourses*.

In chapter 8 of the *Prince*, Machiavelli distinguishes between cruelty well used and cruelty when it is abused. He states:

> Well-used cruelty (if one can speak well of evil) one may call those atrocities that are committed at a stroke, in order to secure one's power, and are not repeated, rather every effort is made to ensure one's subjects benefit in the long run.[47]

---

[46] A.J. Parel, "Machiavelli's Notion of Justice: Text and Analysis," *Political Theory* 18(4) (Nov., 1990) 532.

[47] *Nicollo Machiavelli: Selected Political Writings*, David Wooton, trans. (Indianapolis, MN: Hackett Publishing Company, 1994) 30.

We see here that the purpose of using cruelty is to maintain power. If the government felt that there is a group of dissidents (within the state or outside of the state), it would be in the best interest of the prince to have them executed as soon as possible, and in one quick stroke, meaning that they should all be killed at the same time. Why deal with the problem in one quick stroke? The reason is because the public will quickly forget about atrocities that happen in a short amount of time than one that happens over a long stretch of time. The public will think that the prince was only attacking the dissidents because they were an immediate threat to the principality, and that it is common sense to eliminate one's enemies to maintain power and control. What throws the reader off is that he also mentions the use of cruelty is justified when it benefits one's subjects in the long run. This is hinting that the public interest is also a determining factor. The dissidents might cause social instability, and even lead to further atrocities if the authorities do not deal with them quickly and efficiently. We will find that in the *Discourses*, Machiavelli uses the public interest more often as a way of justifying evil, while the *Prince* focuses more on the retention of power.

The next question is when is the use of cruelty regarded as being an abuse? It is an abuse when it leads to more bloodshed in the long-term rather than less. This can happen, among other things, if a government exploits a foreign country for natural resources, uses that country to establish a military presence to maintain global dominance, or set up a puppet government to maintain control over that country. The U.S. government has been doing this throughout history, and numerous "blowbacks" have resulted including terrorist attacks on U.S. territory and personnel abroad. September 11, 2001 did not happen without any sort of justification.[48] No one is insane enough to fly into a building just for fun. When the U.S. government continues to use force (either military or in the form of economic sanctions), they are instigating trouble and bloodshed in

---

[48] In a speech shortly after the terrorist attack, President George W. Bush had the indecency to tell the people of this nation to go back to their old lifestyle as if nothing happened; to discourage any attempt at reflecting upon the causes behind such a significant event in U.S. history. As if there weren't enough deaths already, U.S. retaliates in the coming months by sending bombers to Afghanistan to kill the Taliban who are hiding in the caves. Along with their deaths, 3,000 innocent Afghanis (entitled "collateral damage") also died as a result of the bombing.

the near and distant future. The quick and decisive invasion of Iraq to oust the prior U.S. supported Saddam Hussein regime has not tamed the world of U.S. hatred, and there will likely be more terrorist attacks on the U.S. and its allies.[49] The initial attack on Iraq achieved its goal (to remove Saddam's regime) in a short amount of time, but the bloodshed continues in Iraq against U.S. military soldiers, foreign aid workers, and Iraqi citizens. Machiavelli would not have supported this recent invasion and occupation of Iraq because it has created more bloodshed, rather than less, and thus it is an abuse of cruelty. The best way for the U.S. government to prevent future terrorist attacks is for them to stop conducting terrorist atrocities against other states. But the untamed beast does not want to change its ways because its self-interests are more important than rights, justice, equality, peace, as well as human survival and environmental stability. The United States government is known to preach one way, but act in other. The same standards do not apply to this government. In describing the lawless behavior like that of the animal kingdom, let us now examine Machiavelli's analogy of the fox and the lion.

One major difference between the animal kingdom and human society is that we have laws and animals do not. Laws provide order within society, which is why Machiavelli stresses the importance of having good laws in addition to having good armies. Laws are also required to habituate people into behaving properly. Without laws, people can become ruthless and cause anarchy. But it is sometimes necessary for the prince to act like a beast by not following the laws in order to win, and lying and acting in other immoral ways when necessary. There is an important passage where he talks about this:

> A ruler, and particularly a ruler who is new to power, cannot conform to all those rules that men who are thought good are expected to respect, for he is often obliged, in order to hold on to power, to break his word, to be uncharitable, inhumane, and irreligious. So he must be mentally prepared to act as circumstances and changes in fortune require. As I have said, he

---

[49] The U.S. supplied Hussein with weapons of mass destruction in the 1980's. The use of biological weapons on the people of Iran and the northern Iraqi Kurds were used under the full knowledge of the U.S. government.

should do what is right if he can; but he must be prepared to do wrong when necessary.[50]

There are several key ideas that are worthwhile to explore within this passage. The first is that the prince has an obligation to hold onto power, therefore he must do whatever it takes to maintain his power including lying and breaking the law. We must remember that justice (in the normal sense of the word) is not a part of Machiavelli's notion of virtue, and therefore it is okay to perform these acts in order to maintain his notion of positive justice. It is therefore necessary for the prince to act like a human by following the laws when it is appropriate, but the prince must also be cunning like a fox and ferocious like a lion when it will help him win. Also in the passage, Machiavelli mentions that the prince should act appropriately in changing times, and also when fortune requires. This is how one achieves control over the environment. It's a pragmatic justification to explain the behavior of a good prince. This passage also explains why the U.S. government must act above the law in order to maintain global power. No other entity, neither the International Court nor the U.N. Security council, can put a stop to this ruthless behavior because no entity has enough force to tame this beast. This government has military supremacy over any other state in the world, which is why it can exert its force on others in order to maintain power.

Machiavelli would probably be in favor of having a strong military presence, but this government must also be careful with its foreign policy in order to prevent future blowbacks. The power of this government would likely be diminished if they lack moderation. Up to this point, I have not seen any significant changes in the U.S. government's policies, both domestic and abroad. Hatred against this government both abroad and from within will grow, which will cause more unpopularity and more violence in this world. If the U.S. wants to maintain its power, it must change its political agenda towards self-destruction. Power is also spoken in monetary terms. The U.S. must also re-establish its ability to produce goods domestically, instead of exporting most of the manufacturing to other countries. Since China has this advantage, it will likely become the next superpower, while the power of the U.S. will decline. The Pentagon will not be able to maintain its average annual budget of $450 billion if our

---

[50] Ibid. 53.

economy is weak and if it has a growing deficit. If the federal government has less money, it will not be able to continue funding the Pentagon at such a high rate, and it will also not be able to fund and invest in other areas of society such as education and health care. This becomes a vicious cycle because the fuel that allows this government to operate comes from the taxpayers of this country. In chapter 19 of the *Prince*, Machiavelli writes about how the populace of Rome wants peace and quiet and their ruler to be unassuming. The current state of affairs in this country is not like this. For this reason, government support will likely to decline, and along with it, the money to maintain global military dominance. The idea of holding onto power is also prevalent in the *Discourses*. Let us now examine the use of evil and extralegal methods in this latter text.

Justification of Evil Acts in the *Discourses*

The notion of power is still important in the *Discourses*, but instead of having a principality, Machiavelli promotes the idea of having a republic. He also stresses the public good to justify the actions of the legislature. In Chapter 9 of the *Discourses*, he argues that power should be concentrated under one legislature when establishing a new republic or reforming an old one. This will allow for the establishment of a good institution. Elsewhere, Machiavelli discuses about how in the Roman Empire, it was sometimes necessary for the senate to hand over the power to one person in order to solve the problem of gridlock due to the disagreements among the ruling members. This powerful legislature should do whatever it takes to organize the republic, including extralegal actions. He states:

> "A wise man will never criticize someone for an extralegal action undertaken to organize kingdom or establish a republic."[51]

The establishment of a republic is a good course of action. Violence used to "create anew" is justified, while violence used to destroy is not. A descriptive example is given in Chapter 26 of the *Discourses* where he states that a new ruler of a city or territory should establish everything

---

[51] Ibid. 108.

anew in order to gain power, whether it is to set up a monarchy or a republic:

> [H]e should build new cities and destroy those that already exist. He should move populations from one place to another. In short, he should leave nothing as it was in the whole territory. There should be no office, no rank, no authority, no wealth which is not acknowledge[d] by its possessor as being his gift.[52]

Once again, we see that maintaining power is more important than anything else. I don't see why this has to be the case. If the ruler gets the people on his side, the people can be used to help re-establish the society. The existing population would have to follow the new laws established by the legislature. It only seems necessary to deal with certain segments of the population to insure the power of the new ruler. Furthermore, if the newly acquired territory has a large population, it can bring in a large amount of tax revenue for the newly established republic. Once again, I don't believe that a great deal of injustice is required for the new ruler to gain power and to establish a new republic. Nevertheless, Machiavelli argues that a ruler should and can do anything it takes to gain all the power, and then use that power to build a republic, and this is supposedly the ultimate good.

The good of the collective society is also emphasized in Chapter 41 of the *Discourses*:

> If you are discussing nothing less than the safety of the homeland, then you should pay no attention to what is just or what is unjust, or to what is kind or cruel, or to what is praiseworthy or shameful. You should put every other consideration aside, and you should adopt wholeheartedly the policy most likely to save your homeland's life and preserve her liberty.[53]

Nationalism is more important than individual liberty, which is why a ruler of a state should do whatever it takes to obtain and retain power. This is required in order to establish a good republic. A republic also needs its own military to protect the state from foreign invasion. This military

---

[52] Ibid. 131.

[53] Ibid. 215.

should consist of its own citizens. People who are fighting to defend their own property are more loyal to the ruler than mercenary or foreign troops.[54] Protecting national security is a good reason for the government to further limit individual liberty. What they are really doing in our government is protecting the interests of the ruling elite and the other entities such as the military industrial complex. They're fighting a war against terrorism because their own terrorist acts against other states have resulted in blowback. The same government officials who preach democracy and liberty are also the same people who are willing to lie to the public, manipulate the voting process, kill innocent men, women, and children, and overthrow democratically elected officials to promote their own self-interests. It's not really about the national security of the nation, but the security of these ruling entities within our country. They do not respect the liberty of individuals in other countries. Why should they respect individual liberty in this country? Machiavelli would be against this since it is not really in the interest of the country, but a selected few.

Conclusion

Machiavelli is in favor of using evil tactics to gain power for the ruler and to protect the homeland security and liberty. These evil methods must be used with caution because they can result in retaliation. These methods do not protect individual rights, justice, and equality. A more favorable approach would be to gain power through the popularity of the people. If the majority of the people favor the ruler of their country, they are more likely to do what the leaders says. Support by the majority will also make it difficult for anyone else to take over the rule of the land.

Humans have the capability to be more rational than animals. They should use rationality to keep themselves out of trouble and to promote the public good. It is in the interest of humans to promote self-preservation. If evil forces within this world continue to act lawlessly like the animal kingdom to profit from the destruction and exploitation of others, they will eventually bring about their own destruction simply because they neither posses unlimited powerful nor unlimited resources, and because the majority of the world are against them. The American Empire may fall one day due to its ruthless acts of terror against other

---

[54] See the *Prince*, Chapter 13, and the *Discourses*, Chapter 20.

states, its hypocritical doctrine of "appropriate" behavior, and its control and manipulation of the public interest. The dominant forces are too selfish to learn from history. Using rationality to promote peace, justice, equality, rights, and liberty will ensure the survival of the human species for many generations. Ruthless violence may insure immediate power and control, but for how long can violence and oppression control the majority of the exploited and dominated members of this world? Long-term stability is more favorable than short-term stability, therefore methods that will achieve the former should be chosen over the latter.

Part II: Theories of Governance

Chapter 7:
Arguments in Favor and Against Strong and Centralized Government

Introduction

In mid-February of 2003, roughly 150,000 people gathered in San Francisco to protest against going to war with Iraq. On the same weekend, millions more around the world also protested against possible U.S. and British invasion of Iraq, of which would occur a month later. France proposed to veto any U.N. Security Council resolution proposed by the United States to go to war with Iraq. Shortly thereafter, the U.S. government decided to go to war with Iraq, along with Britain, without the consent of the U.N. Security Council, and against the voices of millions of protesters. Is the executive branch to powerful for its own good? Is the voice of the people adequately represented? This chapter sets out to explore the original arguments by those who favored a strong, centralized government (the federalists) and those who were against it (the anti-federalists) prior to the adoption of the U.S. constitution and the union of the thirteen original states.

Arguments from the Federalists

The Federalists were in favor of one centralized government and not merely a confederation with each state running its own affairs. An influential document to the constitution was the Virginia Resolutions of 1787, which was in favor of having a national government. Section three states that the legislature should be divided into two branches in order to weaken this branch of government. Madison in the *Federalist Papers* number 50 concurred. In section 9 of the Virginia Resolutions, it proposes the establishment of a supreme tribunal:

> Resd. that the National Judiciary be established to consist of one or more supreme tribunals, and of inferior tribunals to be chosen by the National Legislature, to hold their offices during good behavior....[55]

---

[55] "The Virginia Resolutions" in *The Origin of the American Constitution: A documentary History*, Michael Kammen, ed. (New York: Penguin Books, 1986), 24.

Of course, we only ended up having one supreme tribunal. The resolutions also wanted an executive chosen by the national legislature, but instead, it's chosen by our Electoral College. Nevertheless, this document was influential to the constitution, and it broke away from the mere confederation that was presented in the Articles of Confederation.

Madison was afraid that in a republican government, the legislative branch would have too much power. And for this reason, he explains the method of weakening it in the *Federalist Papers* number 50:

> The remedy for this inconveniency is, to divide the legislature into different branches; and to render them by different modes of election, and different principles of actions, as little connected with each other....[56]

In addition to this, "an absolute negative", or a veto, should be given to the executive to increase its power in relation to the legislative branch. All of this is applicable today. The division in the legislative branch slows down the entire process because of the necessary approval of both houses. This is exactly what Madison wanted because he believed that promptitude in the legislative process is a bad thing. In the *Federalist Papers* number 70, he explains that the differences of opinion will allow for a constructive discussion and it acts as a check on the majority. Also in number 70, Madison discusses about the notion of *energy* in the executive branch. One of the primary roles of the President is to protect the country from foreign invasion, and therefore the executive branch must possess a tremendous amount of power to be able to fulfill this task. Madison also states, "A feeble executive implies a feeble execution of the government."[57] In order for the executive branch to fulfill its responsibility with efficiency, it must be given the strength, or energy, to do so. But Madison's notion of a powerful executive also implies that it is able to abuse its power to fulfill the interests of those in power, and not necessary what is best for the nation. An example would be the executive branch using military force when it thinks is necessary, such as the war on Iraq sought by the second Bush Administration, even though millions of people were against this. My argument is that the powers of the executive should be used in a

---

[56] Ibid. 204.

[57] Ibid. 220.

responsible manner. One reason why it has not is because of its overwhelming amount of power. Let us now explore the arguments against having a centralized government and the tremendous power that are given to each branch from the perspective of the anti-federalists.

Arguments from the Anti-Federalists

The anti-federalists were against having a centralized government in the first place. The Articles of Confederation was the legitimate document of the union for a short time. It states that each state will continue to have its executive, legislative, and judicial powers. Undermining these, as was proposed in the Constitution, would undermine the sovereignty and autonomy of each state. It also states that any changes that are to be made to the Article must be approved unanimously by all 13 states. Once the Constitution replaced the Articles of the Confederation, only the consent of 9 states was required, which undermined the original agreement. In addition to this, the creation of the Constitution at the convention held in Philadelphia has been criticized as being undemocratic. Let us explore why.

The Dissent of the Pennsylvania Minority written in 1787 explained why the development of the Constitution was undemocratic in nature. It was held for four months behind closed doors, and members were under oath of secrecy. There were even threats against the opponents of the constitution:

> While every measure was taken to intimidate the people against opposing it, the public papers teemed with the most violent threats against those who should dare to think for themselves....[58]

Whatever happened to the consent and representation of the people? In the Constitution of Philadelphia, any proposed changes to be made to the state's constitution must be shown to the public in order for proper examination and criticisms. This did not happen for the newly proposed

---

[58] "Dissent of the Pennsylvania Minority (1787)" in *American Political Thought*, Kenneth M. Dolbeare, ed. (Chatham, NJ: Chatham House Publisher, 1998), 131.

Constitution of the United States, which would eventually undermine the constitution of Pennsylvania.

The dissenting minority was against the Constitution for two main reasons, both of which rested on the notion of consolidation. An expansive territory cannot be governed as effectively by a consolidated governmental structure as a more local one can. Furthermore, it will undermine freedom:

> [A] very extensive territory cannot be governed on the principles of freedom, otherwise than by a confederation of republics, possessing all the powers of internal government, but united in the management of their general and foreign concerns.[59]

This goes back to Montesquieu's discussion of how a republic is best managed if it is small. In a republic, certain elected officials represent the affairs of the people. The smaller the population, the smaller the ratio between each representative and the total number of people. This is a big problem within our government today. One can argue that the federal government should be more representative of the nation since we have such a large number of people. It is not fair for one person to speak on behalf of so many because the opinions of the many become diluted in the voices of the few representatives. Furthermore, one can also argue that we should elect our representatives in each of the three branches of government more directly than the approach that we have to today. Three tiers divide the election between our President and the people (the President is elected by the Electoral College, and these members are chosen by members of each state legislature, and the state legislature is elected by the people). This filtration process can undermine the authenticity of representation because each level can dilute and filter out the interests of the people. What ends up happening is the consolidation of power in the hands of a few people that are able to make major decisions affecting the entire nation. They do not always act from the general will of the people. This consolidation was the other fear held by the Pennsylvania minority:

> We dissent, secondly, because the powers vested in Congress by this constitution, must necessarily annihilate and absorb the legislative,

---

[59] Ibid. 135.

executive, and judicial powers of the several States, and produce from their ruins one consolidate government, which from the nature of things will be *an iron handed despotism*, as nothing short of the supremacy of despotic sway could connect and govern these United States under one government....[60]

Elbridge Gerry, who was elected to the Massachusetts House of Representative in 1786, also criticized the lack of representation and the powers held by each branch. He stated that the powers of the executive are blended in with the legislative, which is exactly what we have today. Since the Vice President is required to be of the same political party as the President, and since the Vice President is also the President of the Senate, he sets the agenda on the legislative process and holds back other agendas that he or the Executive apposes. We have in essence an executive branch manipulating the legislative process. For this reason, the powers of the executive branch should be weakened to hand back most of the legislative power back to where it should belong, Congress. He also feared the oppression of the judicial branch. This is clearly understandable since there are so few members, and since it is the President who nominates these officials, with the consent of the Senate. The majority of the people should have say on who is to be on the Supreme Court simply because the decisions made by this court will have a tremendous effect on the laws of this land, of which will trickle down to every member of this country. Why should we let an official, who is not even representative of the people, be allow to have so much power over this? It is surely not representative, nor democratic.

George Mason also brought up the same criticisms with regards to a lack of representation and the mix of powers that the executive has with the legislative. He criticizes the House of Representatives as being only a "shadow" representation of the people, but I do not think this is really the case since they are voted directly by the people. However, we ought to have greater representation because of our large population. Mason also criticizes the combined power of the executive and the legislature as destabilizing the balance:

---

[60] Ibid.

These with their other great Powers (vizt. their Power in the Appointment of Ambassadors and all public Officers, in making Treaties, and in trying all Impeachments) their Influence upon and Connection with the supreme Executive from these Causes, their Duration of Office, and their being a constant existing Body almost continually sitting, joined with their being one [complete] Branch of the Legislature, will destroy any Balance in the Government, and enable them to accomplish what Usurpations they please upon the Rights and Libertys of the People.[61]

This further supports the argument that the powers of these two branches should be limited. To keep certain officials, such as the Senators, from holding on to too much power, I propose that their terms be limited to allow a greater rotation.

Conclusion

There is a large disparity between the poor and the rich within this country. Those who are elected into the executive branch or the legislative branch tend to be from a rather privileged background. For this reason, most do not really represent the average American worker, which is why the people of this country should directly vote for these officials instead of having other officials elect them for us. Money, greed, and power are factors that underlie politics, which is another reason why the average person ought to play a more important role in politics, such as running for political office, electing a government official, or supporting a campaign to make sure that our government is acting out of the interest of the general good, and not for special interest. There is a correlation that comes with having a tremendous amount of wealth, and that correlation is power. When these wealthy individuals dominate public office, they will gain even more influence and control over their own interests, and they are able to make public policy that will often affect the entire nation and even the entire world. When these powers are abused, such as taking a country to war when millions of people are against it, it undermines the legitimacy of our supposedly representative and partially democratic government. An abuse in these powers can also result in the suffering or death of a large group of people within this world. All of these reasons supports the argument that certain changes should be made to the three branches of our

---

[61] Ibid. 256.

government in order to reduce these tyrannical actions of those who play an important role in the management of the state, and ultimately in the management of our lives. The power of this government should be handed back to the same people who it is supposed to serve and to protect.

Chapter 8:
Changes in Governance

Introduction

The purpose of this chapter is to provide a discussion of new forms of governance and the affects leading up to it. The interconnectedness of the world has led to changes in governance to effectively manage the social, economic, and political changes. If left unimpeded, there will be a natural strive towards efficiency, just like the efficiency of the free market. This new form of governance is pluralistic and democratic in nature.

I will begin by giving a preliminary discussion of governance – what it is and how we arrived from a state-centered form of governance to a decentralized one that involves multiple actors, both private and public. I will then discuss the factors that have led and will continue to lead to new forms of governance. I will then explore the new forms of governance and the problems that it faces in the existing literature.

Background Information

What first needs to be addressed is the notion of governance. The term itself is considered to be persuasive and has different meanings. Some of the different types of governance are corporate governance, good governance, collaborate governance, risk governance, and global governance. I choose to define governance as the rules, regulations, and management style of a given entity to fulfill a certain goal. The best form of governance is one that achieves the end goal in the most efficient manner, but also in a way that takes human values into consideration such as working together to achieve equality, rights, and justice. Democracy is achieved based on the pluralistic nature of governance – often having multiple actors working together to achieve a common goal and these multiple actors act as a check and balance on each other through the deliberation and collaboration process.

It would be helpful to understand the theory behind what used to be a popular form of governance – state-centered or centralized governance. The theory that led up to this is that society will fall apart unless there is a strong, centralized authority managing the day-to-day aspects of society. People are too selfish to work together to achieve a common end, and for this reason, there has to be a higher authority to take care of the public's needs and to act as an overseer. But it turns out that too much centralized control often leads to inefficiency. A good example would be the economic system. Many now favor a less centralized form of market system – that of the free market, because it is the most efficient form of system that results in the best prices for consumers due to competition and innovation. This process is natural because these are the end goals that we want to achieve in the market system. The same argument can be applied in other areas such as the management of society. There has been a trend towards a less decentralized form of governance, taken on by multiple actors, both private and public ones, to achieve a more efficient way of arriving at the end goal. I argue that this is a natural process because it is better to achieve the same goal with the least amount of resources possible while maintaining accountability and transparency. A multitude of private actors have emerged to take over many of the functions of the public actor. The state now takes on a stirring rather than a rowing function. That is, the government these days has only enough power to stir or help guide public policy rather than dictate policy because other agencies, both government and non-government agencies, also undertake this task as well – no one single institution has ultimate authority. Nonetheless, the state continues to grow to keep up with the development and complexity of the world, and for this reason, it still has a very important function to play.

Factors Leading to New Forms of Governance

The most apparent factor leading to a change in governance is the trend towards achieving efficiency. This includes cutting back unnecessary resources such as time and cost. There has been a trend from rule-based to results-based because in the end, it is about achieving the desired outcome. A common structural problem that leads to inefficiency is the nature of traditional style management, particularly top-down or hierarchical system of management. A detailed discussion on this issue will be provided later on.

Another leading factor of the new style of governance is due to globalization. David Held describes globalization as the "stretching or intensification of social, economic and political relations across regions and continents."[62] The world is becoming more and more interconnected.

---

[62] David Held, "Regulating Globalization? The Reinvention of Politics," *International Sociology*, 14 (2) (2002): 395.

New information technology has enabled us to send vast amounts of information, such as news, across the entire globe. A remote part of Asia can see and hear what is going on in the United States and vice versa. We are thus influenced by other people in other cultures through communications technology such as the television, the telephone, and the internet. Another sign of the interconnectedness of the world is that of the financial market. The financial market is linked through information technology. Currency can be transferred and traded globally in a matter of seconds. Goods, services, and investments can also be purchased in the same manner. But this has led to an interdependence of the market. If there is a financial crisis in one region of the world, such as Southeast Asia, it can have a profound effect on the entire global financial market. Another way our world is boundless is on certain important issues such as global warming. The massive amounts of carbon dioxide and other green house gases will affect the global and not just the regional climate. For this reason, the industrialized countries must collaborate with one another to keep global warming under control. An important common interest is at stake. There is also a need for regulation to manage neomercantilism. Things such as strategic trade and intellectual property rights must be protected, and this must be done on an international scale, which leads to the necessity of having international regulating agencies. Regulation also helps to legitimize markets and helps to facilitates transactions by enhancing trust among multiple actors.

Global interdependence leads to non-traditional, non-unilateral ways of solving problems. Both public and private actors must work together to arrive at an efficient way of achieving goals, which can be too difficult to achieve unilaterally. Globalization also effects democracy. It leads to multilateral sources of power, a larger scale of society and of government, a diffusion of power, and it leads to the new boundary problem. A new system of governance emerges to cope with these issues.

The New World of Governance

Common Attributes

Before discussing in detail about the different forms of governance that have shown up in the existing literature, I would like to discuss the important attributes of the new form of decentralized governance. It is decentralized because there are multiple actors involved, which may or may not include public actors. Multiple actors often work together to share resources such as information. Together, these actors form a network. To help achieve accountability, these agencies ought to be transparent – the day-to-day activities including its accounting practices ought to be made available to the public. The issue of accountability in the new form of governance is problematic as we will see later on. It is common for management to be bottom-up instead of top-down because ordinary people have a greater say in the operations and in the policy making process. It is also a horizontal style of management because multiple actors are involved, working together and sharing resources and information to achieve a goal. This newer form of governance also usually involves the local community, and it is also problem centered. There is a clear and practical problem that needs to be addressed, and the goal is to achieve it in the most efficient way possible. There is also a shift from the traditional rule-based style of management to a results-based style of management. Once again, the emphasis is on whether or not the goal is being achieved in the best possible manner. Let us now explore the various aspects of this new form of governance.

Networks

Governance, since it often involves multiple actors, can be described as a network. Mark Schneider states that networks form the core of governing structures.[63] It is a more horizontal form of organization with each actor playing an important role. Networks can also be characterized as having high levels of interdependence and multiple levels of organization. As a result, the formal lines of authority are blurred. What was commonly centralized control is now dispersed.

Networks stimulate collaboration and cooperation in several ways. First, it promotes deliberation. Since there are multiple actors, they must learn how to work together to achieve a common goal. Private actors will

---

[63] Mark Schneider et al., "Building Consensual Institutions: Networks and the National Estuary Program," *American Journal of Political Science*, 47 (1) (2003): 143 – 158.

have a say while working with public actors. It also encourages the people who are affected by regulation to be involved. What was traditionally a hierarchical command and control style of management now becomes a bottom-up and horizontal style of management. The entire process becomes a cooperative process, rather than an adversarial one; it is more democratic and less authoritative.

There are several key factors that lead to the success of networks. The first comes from individuals making "mutually beneficial exchanges and agreements that otherwise would not take place."[64] The second comes from the sharing of resources, such as the sharing of information. The third is the increase of commitments to fulfill the agreements, which results in higher creditability for these actors. The main constraints of these networks are the costs associated with development and maintaining contacts.

New Public Management Model (NPM)

Now that we have examined the basic underlying structure of this newer interdependent, networked, and decentralized form of governance, we can focus on more specific models of governance. A new style of management to reflect the new world of governance is called New Public Management (NPM). NPM has several goals in mind. The first is to apply the corporate model to increase efficiency. The second is to take existing groups and make them more efficient. The third is to create autonomous agencies to respond to market forces. The overall goal of NPM is to make the state more efficient.

The primary reason for NPM is due to the inefficiency of the public sector. The public sector does not respond to market forces like the private sector does. It is also not responsive to the public. For these reasons, there is very little incentive for the public sector to change in order to be more efficient. NPM creates market-like conditions such as contracting out services, productively is measured by the outcome, more control is given to managers and accountability falls on them, reward and punishment is based on performance, and agencies are freed up so that they can hire and fire as they please. A major shift is the focus on outputs rather than inputs. The output is the thing that is done to achieve the goal, or the outcome,

---

[64] Ibid. 144.

and this is what is being measured. The emphasis is therefore whether or not the end goal is achieved and how successful it has been achieved.

NPM faces a serious problem. Measuring the outcome is problematic because it is a difficult task and it could lead to unintended consequences. An example would be the standardized test in secondary school. These tests are administered with the intention of measuring the teaching effectiveness of each school, and ultimately of each teacher. What can end up happening is that the teacher will then focus his or her style of teaching in order to live up to these tests, which can undermine a more valuable kind of education that is being given to the students.

Empowered Participatory Governance (EPG)

Another form of governance that has emerged is called empowered participatory governance (EPG). In this case, ordinary people in a local community have control over governance. Therefore, EPG is a decentralized form of governance. One of several examples given in the Fung and Wright article is the governance of public schools in Chicago.[65] These schools were some of the poorest performing schools in the nation. The state decided to try something new, and that was to give each local community control over the management of the schools. Concerned parents and teachers came together to figure out what was effective and what needed to be changed. The end effect was a large improvement over the quality of these schools. The basic criticism of top-down management or centralized control, especially in this case, is that management is too disassociated from what they are managing. Since they do not have firsthand experience of the situation, they end up making bad management decisions.

There are three principles in EPG: practical orientation, bottom-up participation, and deliberative solution generation. All are effective for obvious reasons, but the source leading to its effectiveness also leads to problems. This form of participatory governance is "vulnerable to [a]

---

[65] See Archon Fung and Erik Olin Wright, "Thinking about Empowered Participatory Governance," in *Deepening Democracy: Institutional Innovations in Empowered Participatory Governance* (San Francisco: Analytical Psychology Club of San Francisco, 2003), pp. 3 – 42.

serious problem of power and domination inside deliberative arenas by powerful factions or elites."[66] This is a good criticism, but one that should not be taken too seriously. Anytime a group of people get together to achieve a common goal, there is bound to be difference of opinion and a power struggle among the contenders, but this is the result of democracy. The greater the diversity of people and their opinions, the less likely there will be a concentration of power. And even if there is domination by one group, it will be open to scrutiny by other members. Let us now explore some of the challenges facing the new world of governance.

Problems Facing the New World of Governance

The first issue I would like to talk about relates to the last criticism about the domination of elite forces. Jo Beall raises this criticism while writing on the issue of decentralization and international development.[67] Beall argues that decentralization is a core component of international development. The positive benefit of decentralization is that it improves accountably, transparency, and state-society relations. The negative consequence of decentralization is that it can lead to elite capture, toward pork-barrel politics, and local governments can be deprived of human and financial resources to cope with the demands of centralization, as was the case with South Africa. Beall also states that deregulation does not work well in rural areas because 1.) they are more traditionalists and 2.) rural areas are poorer, therefore they provide less revenue for the government.

More general problems about regulation include the fact that regulations adds to the cost for industries, and the consumers will likely pick up these costs if the industries want to retain more profits. But consumers are willing to pay only so much for a product before they decide to purchase the same or similar product by another manufacturer at a more affordable price. As markets continue to expand, more regulation will be required to keep these markets operating efficiently.

---

[66] Ibid. 33.

[67] Jo Beall, "Decentralizing Government and Decentralizing Gender: Lessons from Local Government Reform in South Africa," *Politics and Society*, 33 (2) (2003): 253-276.

Another key issue is on the issue of legitimization. States need to legitimate their actions through science, which leads to "risk analysis". But the problem with risk analysis is that it can become politicized, such as the example with the FDA. This also raises the question as to whether or not all forms of regulatory agencies can operate without the coercion and influence of outside forces such as business or politics. In the case of the FDA, the answer is no. The same people who they were watching over also provided them with funding. They are also subject to a social and ethical dilemma – the side effects and effectiveness of new drugs cannot truly be determined until it has been given to the general public. In a scientific study, the greater the number of participants involved in the study, the more reliable the study will become. The pharmaceutical companies only conduct a study based on several thousands of people. Nevertheless, there is pressure to get these drugs onto the open market because they have the potential of creating greater utility, such has helping people with harmful conditions, than resulting in negative ones, such as death. The dilemma the FDA faces is whether they should hold ethical standards above maximizing utility or the other way around.

Conclusion

Anne-Marie Slaughter states that it is paradoxical that we want and need more government on a regional and global scale, but at the same time we want less centralized control and coercive authority that takes power away from the people that are being governed.[68] Institutions are beneficial, but they can also be oppressive. It is further complicated by the concern of accountability. The solution that she offers is having government networks because it is a pluralist form of governance that will increase transparency, accountability, the sharing of resources, and most importantly, it will promote democratic principles such as deliberation and cooperation to achieve a common goal. It is also important that the people affected by regulation are involved in the regulation process. The end goal of the state is to provide services for its citizens in the most efficient manner as possible without undermining the quality of service. Private actors are often able to perform this function better than public ones. For this reason,

---

[68] Anne-Marie Slaughter, *A New World Order* (New Jersey: Princeton University Press, 2005).

the private sector is becoming more involved and has a greater say in public policy. They are the "rowers" and the states are now the "stirrers" because NGOs are becoming a dominant driving force of public policy and governments of states play a more passive role of guiding public policy along a certain path just like a boat propeller guides a boat into a certain direction. Just like the market system, there will be a natural strive towards greater efficiency, because to do so is to achieve the function of management in a more excellent manner. What is better is more desirable and in this case, it is the desire to have a more efficient form of local, regional, and global governance. This is the reason why a new form of governance has replaced the old one. In the Darwinian sense, the fit has outlived the unfit.

Chapter 9:
Challenges Facing Global Civil Society

Introduction

Representative and multi-lateral political organizations such as the United Nations try their best to deal with important issues affecting the global community, but they face the problem of having conflicting goals and ideologies, which is the result of pluralism. This can be observed even among the five permanent members of the United Nations Security Council. An example would be the recent decision of the U.S. government to violate a sovereign country, Iraq, arguably to fulfill the interests of those in power. Global civil society, because it is on a global scale, faces the problem of universal consent and mutual agreement. It also lacks a central executive and military power to help maintain its complex, global cosmocracy, and to uphold international law. In this chapter, I will argue that it is not possible to achieve a global civil society.

Characteristics of Civil Society

In his book *Global Civil Society*, John Keane provides us with five central characteristics of global civil society as outlined below:

1. Global civil society consists of "non-governmental structures and activities. It comprises individuals, households, profit-seeking businesses, not-for-profit non-governmental organizations, coalitions, social movements and linguistic communities and cultural identities."[69]

2. Global civil society is a society that is dynamically interlinked. Global civil society has emergent properties that cannot be found by merely adding the sum of its parts, which is why Keane describes it as being "neither an organism nor a mechanism".

3. Global civil society consists of civility. People must be polite towards strangers, and they must accept the fact that they are living in a heterogeneous society, which consists of different ideologies, religions, ethnicities, and the like. This society also contains pockets

---

[69] John Keane, *Global Civil Society* (Cambridge, UK: Cambridge UP, 2003), 8.

of incivility – "geographic areas that coexist uneasily with 'safe' and highly 'civil' zones...."[70] Global civil society has a strong tendency to strive towards non-violence, mutual respect, cooperation, and even power sharing.

4. Global civil society "contains both strong traces of *pluralism* – and strong *conflict potential*."[71] This is partly the result of its size, heterogeneity, and complex governance.

5. Global civil society spans across all state boundaries.

The information network that expands across the global forum plays an important role in shaping public opinion. Satellite media provides live coverage of important events occurring around the world. This further builds up a sense of community because it brings the world closer to us. The media outlet can also be used to promote propaganda in order to influence the public conscience. It is also used as an advertising medium to promote superficial wants to encourage capital accumulation and material consumption, which are driving forces underlying capitalism. The media itself is not a problem. The problem is when it becomes a monopoly and is used to control the populace. Another criticism is that access to the media and communication is not universal; not every household in the world possesses internet access, a telephone line, or a television set. They would have to rely upon other forms of media, such as newspapers, if they can afford to buy one, but newspapers do not give them live coverage of the news.

On the positive side, global civil society allows civilians to protect their rights by setting limits on the government, and by constantly keeping a watch over them. Power sharing and power checking occur across political boundaries. People living in the United States can get the latest news on the international community, and the international community can also get the latest news on the events occurring within the United States. In a global civil society, when one group commits atrocities, there will likely be an outcry from the international community. When atrocities or natural

---

[70] Ibid. 13.

[71] Ibid. 14.

disasters occur, non-government organizations (NGOs), such as the Red Cross, will quickly respond to the aid of its victims.

Global civil society allows a great deal of freedom, but this means that certain individuals and groups, such as organized gangs, can use it to conduct violence in order to advance their own interests, and thus causing incivility. It is possible for a stronger group to exploit a weaker group in order to fulfill selfish interests, such as the acquisition of power, wealth, or natural resources. These abusive activities must be restrained by an authoritative agency on behalf of the community, but in order to enforce peace and stability, these agencies must also resort to force and violence. Violence, even though it sounds paradoxical, is therefore necessary to maintain peace in a global civil society. But having the power to enforce people through the use of violence, especially by a central authority, can get out of control and end up destabilizing society. This can happen if the power lies within the wrong hands.

Turbocapitalism

An important feature of global civil society is the free market economy, which helps maintain the livelihood of those participating in the economic system, but it also degrades those who are abused by it. It is only possible to acquire wealth if a person participates in the market, but not everyone is able to do this, and it is the function of the government to ensure that everyone has access to the mainstream redistribution system, which consists of trade, commerce, and real estate, in order to prosper in life.[72] There is still plenty of economic inequality, even within a wealthy country such as the U.S. The market economy "is a dynamic source of technological innovation, capital investment, productions, distribution and consumption stretched across vast distances."[73] Economic activity is only possible from non-economic activities, such as the creation of homes, the promotion of identity, meaning, and the like.

---

[72] See J. Owens Smith, *The Politics of Ethnic and Racial Inequality: A Systematic Comparative Macro-Analysis from the Colonial Period to the Present* (Dubuque, Iowa: Kendall/Hunt Publishing Company, 2004) 25.

[73] Keane, 14.

A leading catalyst of global civil society is the market force, also known as *turbocapitalism*:

> Turbocapitalism is a species of private enterprise driven by the desire for emancipation from social custom, territorial state interference, taxation restrictions, trade union intransigence and all other external restrictions upon the free movement of capital in search of profit.[74]

In essence, turbocapitalism wants minimal government restrictions to allow large business to accumulate maximum profit, and this often involves the exploitation of workers by paying them extremely low wages. It seeks deregulation, giving businesses greater control over their market practices, which can lead to the effects of monopolization, such as price gouging. This was seen in the past with the Enron scandal, which involved a large group of lawyers, businessmen, and bankers, many of whom were Harvard associates, working together to gain a monopoly over the energy supply of the American public. This is why there must be, at the minimum, some government intervention in order to protect the public interest. Companies under this enterprise also seek tax avoidances. This is already happening as a result of big tax incentives for companies, and also the creation of off shore accounts. As a result of this abusive practice, the American public has to make up for this large gap in tax deficiency, which means more profit for businesses, and less income for the average worker.

Turbocapitalism also promotes artificial meanings through consumption, which is good for the economic system, but it is not necessarily good for this or any other society in the long-term. In essence, individuals are viewed as nothing more than a money-generating organism for the economic system. Capital accumulation and material wealth should not be the values of a global civil society because they are artificial wants that often becomes counter-productive to the human species, and to the rest of the world. If one spends most of his/her time pursuing monetary accumulation in order to acquire material goods, the focus is mostly on the individual, and not the collective good, such as to maintain peace and security in the local, national, and global community. If we want mutual respect and cooperation in a global civil society, the proper moral dispositions should be fostered into the individual at an early age. These

---

[74] Ibid. 67 – 68.

days, children are brought up to consume and to seek immediate gratification. In 1986, we had more high school than shopping malls. We now have twice as many shopping centers (46,438) than high schools (22,180). Seventy percent of us visit malls each week, and this is more than the percentage of people who attend houses of worship. Americans on average spend 6 hours a week shopping and only 45 minutes playing with their kids.[75] Energy concentrated on individualism, monetary wealth, and consumption also distracts the average person away from more important things, such as the political affairs of the local, national, and international community. Since political decisions often trickle down and affect the individual, it is important to pay attention and to get involved in the political arena. Ancient philosophers such as Aristotle and Plato would consider the life of a politician as being a highly noble one because it involves the management of society as a whole. If we care about our lives, we should care about the policies that affect us, including those that determine what we can and cannot do. We certainly do not want policies that would undermine our life, liberty, property, and the pursuit of happiness.

Another criticism of turbocapitalism deals with marginalization. Those who are left out do not reap the benefits of monetary accumulation, or at least not enough of it to sustain a decent livelihood. Keane explains the percentage of marginalization on the stock of foreign capital by the poorest fifth of the world's population:

> According to one estimate, in 1913 the countries in the bottom fifth of income per person receive around 25 per cent of the world's stock of foreign capital, much the same as the countries in the richest fifth. By 1997, the poorest fifth's share was down to under 5 per cent, compared with 36 per cent for the richest fifth.[76]

The majority of the wealth continues to be marginalized into the hands of fewer and fewer people. Turbocapitalist businesses have the power to invest their money in locations that will bring them the most profit. Money

---

[75] See John De Gaaf, David Wann, and Thomas H. Naylor, *Affluenza: The All-Consuming Epidemic* (Berrett-Koehler Publishers, 2005).

[76] Keane, Ibid. 71.

will flow into these areas, and not others, which contributes to inequality and unemployment. It is not within the interest of turbocapitalism to create wealth and equality for everyone if the primary goal is to accumulate the maximum amount of profit. In addition to social values and the market economy, Kean also discusses a third factor that contributes to global civil society, and that is cosmocracy.

Cosmocracy

It is not surprising to realize that NGOs and other non-government actors often work and are influenced by government institutions, and vice versa. The complex interaction of governmental and related institutions that govern society is known as cosmocracy.

> [C]osmocracy is a system of world-wide webs of interdependence – of actions and reactions at a distance, a complex mélange of networks of legal, governmental, police and military interdependence at world-wide distances.[77]

Cosmocracy can contribute to the ideology of global civil society, but it can also add to its problems and challenges. The complex and multi-layered cosmocracy has several fault lines, which can affect the whole system. An individual decision arising from the top, such as the executive branch of the U.S. government can have an enormous global influence. An example would be the recent decision to invade Iraq and to conduct a war on terrorism. This decision alone has increased American hatred by many fundamentalist groups, which is likely to result in more terrorist attacks against this country. It has also influenced the political affairs of other states. It gave an excuse for many nations to exercise greater force to crackdown terrorists within their own country, such as Israeli forces against terrorist activities conducted by the Palestinian side. The proper way for these two untamed beasts would be to stop conducting their own forms of terrorism against those that would undermine their interests.

Cosmocracy faces several other criticisms as well. The first is that there is no global forum for people to express and share their views in

---

[77] Ibid. 98.

order to shape the international community. The closest one is perhaps the General Assembly within the United Nations, but they do not posses any real power, which actually lies within the five permanent members of the Security Council, including the primary bully who likes to give orders instead of following them – the U.S. government. Furthermore, there is no central executive agency to conduct the affairs of the international community. "There are no political parties that campaign globally, on a regular basis, trying to gather support for certain policies among business and non-business NGOs and receptive governments."[78] There are no global opinions polls either. More importantly, there is no global army or police force to establish and maintain peace across all political boundaries. The closest that we have to this is NATO and the UN Security Council, but even they are hesitant to be involved in every single atrocity. They can also end up making bad decisions. The failed UN mission in Mogadishu during 1993 to capture a leading warlord, which led to the death of several U.S. soldiers, kept the UN out of Rwanda in 1994 where at least 800,000 people were killed in 100 days (or roughly 333 murders an hour). Most of those who died were the Tutsi minority, and the remainder was about 50,000 Hutus.[79] Many were hacked to death by machetes. Cosmocracy also lacks secure rules and regulations, especially those that help maintain peace, stability, and to ensure that everyone has equal and easy access to basic rights such as education, health care, and employment.

Cosmocracy also faces the challenge of having a bullish dominant power, the U.S. government, who often vetoes UN Security resolutions to protect or advance its own interests. Only one veto among the five permanent members will undermine a substantive security resolution, such as waging war. Keane states the following:

> The dominant power often operates bullishly, and it does so because its governing class perceive strength as the principal way in which it can secure its flanks and protect its dominant power privileges, if need be by exercising the right of direct intervention into others' affairs.[80]

---

[78] Ibid. 113.

[79] See James Waller, *Becoming Evil: How Ordinary People Commit Genocide and Mass Killing* (New York: Oxford UP, 2002), 230 – 235.

[80] Keane, 119.

The U.S. government often intervenes in the affairs of other states to acquire things such as power, money, and natural resources. They often do so by undermining human rights, international law, and democracy. They also operate jointly with the CIA and militia groups in foreign countries to overthrow their democratically elected officials in order to set up a puppet regime, one that will be an ally to the U.S. government. Their bullish behavior can be seen in the 2003 decision to invade Iraq on the presumption that 1) they possessed weapons of mass destruction, 2) they were an immediate threat to the U.S. security, and 3) they had ties with Al Qaida. Most of their weapons were destroyed in the 1990's, and it is now known that Saddham Hussein had no close ties with Al Qaida. It is also known that the Bush administration had plans to invade Iraq prior to September 11, 2001, which would further undermine any ties that they would have with Al Qaida. Furthermore, the U.S. decided to invade Iraq without the consent of the UN Security Council, which undermines the council's legitimacy. Therefore, the administration's stated intention to invade Iraq does not sound as being their true intention. Millions of people around the world, including about a million in Britain, protested against the use of force, but this did not change the fate of unnecessary military aggression. The military industrial complex and sub-contractors will profit in the occupation, defense, and reconstruction of Iraq. They will continue to make money as long as the U.S. government continues to create, find, or exaggerate new sources of threat. The U.S. has maintained an average of $350 billion on the military, even after the cold war. The terrorist attack of 9-11 is an excuse to spend even more. In a 2007 issue of *Foreign Policy Magazine*, it is estimated that $250,000 per minute is being spent in Iraq.[81]

The U.S. government also sends billions of dollars to Israel, which allows the Israeli government to further undermine and to degrade the Palestinian people in the occupied territories. Israel possesses weapons of mass destruction, including nuclear capabilities, and has the fourth largest military in the world, thanks to the U.S. government. The U.S. wants to extend its military arm via Israel, which means that they will allow them to continue with its state assassinations against Hamas leaders and others

---

[81] *Foreign Policy Magazine*, January / February issue, 2007.

who are deemed as a security threat against the Israeli government and its civil society. Over and over again, we can see that the U.S. is hypocritical in its foreign relations. It preaches human rights, equality, and democracy only to undermine them. It is able to do so only because it has the wealth to maintain the strongest military presence around the world. It does so even against the authority of the UN Security Council and also against millions of people.

The U.S. government, including other states, is able to carry out atrocities because there is no central authority to prohibit tyrannical behavior, which is why the realist school of international relations sees the international arena as being anarchical. Scott Turner states the following in his article on "Global Civil Society, Anarchy and Governance":

> Because the international system is anarchical, with no overarching governmental authority above the state, it is pre-moral. Thus, the actions of states cannot be judged by the moral standards that we apply to individual human beings within states.[82]

States, such as the U.S. government, are able to act above international law, norms, and moral values because there is no "leviathan", or sovereign power, as Hobbes would put it, to uphold these laws and morals with force. This is why state-centric realism will argue that it is not possible to achieve civility in a global civil society. Moral constraint from undermining the livelihood of fellow citizens is a crucial element in such a society. The universal respect of differences is not enough. Having one centralized government and military agency is required to maintain the actions of every state and deviant group, but this can also lead to despotism. The next section will explore the possible implications of having a centralized world power.

The Problem of Centralization

Article II of the Articles of Confederation, which became effective March 1, 1781, states the following:

---

[82] Scott Turner, "Global Civil Society, Anarchy and Governance: Assessing an Emerging Paradigm", *Journal of Peace Research* v 35 (1) (Jan., 1998): 27.

> Each state retains its sovereignty, freedom and independence, and every Power, Jurisdiction and right, which is not by this confederation expressly delegated to the United States, in Congress assembled.[83]

All thirteen states ratified this. Later in 1787, the Virginia Resolutions was presented to the constitutional convention. It suggested the promotion of a national government, which eventually led to the creation of the constitution that we have today. Around this time, two leading federalists, Alexander Hamilton and James Madison, promoted the idea of having a centralized government for the union, which would have supreme executive, legislative, and judicial power over the thirteen states because they feared, among other things, that factions may one day take control of the government and this would undermine the interests of the aristocracy. The anti-federalist criticized that having a centralized government, especially one that has power and control over the entire nation, can lead to an "iron handed despotism". They also believed that governance is more effective on a small scale, not a large one, especially one that would include the entire span of the thirteen states. This was expressed in the Dissent of the Pennsylvania Minority of 1787:

> [A] very extensive territory cannot be governed on the principles of freedom, otherwise than by a confederation of republics, possessing all the powers of internal government, but united in the management of their general and foreign concerns.[84]

Rousseau expressed a similar view on the advantages of small territorial governance over a large one:

> The more the social bond extends the looser it becomes, and in general a small state is proportionately stronger than a large one.[85]

---

[83] "Articles of Confederation" in *American Political Thought*, Kenneth M. Dolbeare, ed. (Chatham, NJ: Chatham House Publisher, 1998), 10.

[84] "Dissent of the Pennsylvania Minority" in Ibid. 135.

[85] Jean-Jacques Rousseau, "On The Social Contract" in *The Basic Political Writings of Jean-Jacques Rousseau* (Indianapolis, Indiana: Hackett Publishing Company, 1987), 167.

He also states that it is important for the populace to see the leader from time to time otherwise they will become disassociated and have less affection for the leader. Having one executive leader for a large country such as the U.S. is bad enough. Imagine having one leader for the entire world.

Management and representation on a small scale such as at the local and state level (in the U.S.) is better because the representatives will be more in touch with their local community, and they can handle the legislative process without the extra bureaucracy that comes with having a centralized government. Imagine all the bureaucracy that would be involved in having one central agency to handle the executive, legislative, and judicial branches of the entire world. Macro-management would be highly complex and it would involve, among other things, a lot of time, channels of communication, diplomacy, paper work, and personnel to fulfill its function. The central governing agency would be far out of reach from many communities and smaller states. For this reason, having a central agency for global civil society will likely impede upon rather than provide for a proper and efficient governance of a global civil society.

Conclusion

Global civil society is an intricate network of "nongovernmental structures and activities". There is also a third factor that contributes to the formation of a global civil society, which is called cosmocracy – the complex web of interdependent forces, including government agencies such as the police and military forces. Government agencies and NGOs are often framed and enabled by each other. Having a central world agency to oversee executive, legislative, judicial functions, and military forces to prevent factions and to keep groups from abusing the freedom that global civil society offers can lead to despotism. Perhaps the best thing to do is to let each state manage its own affairs, and have several alliances, such as NATO, the European Union, and the UN Security Council. This is perhaps a more affective means of governance because it is more democratic, smaller, and easier to manage. NGOs and the international community should continue to exert pressure for every state to comply with human rights and international law. The people of each nation should also prevent potential tyrants and abusers of the political system from going into office.

And for the United States, let us first handle the affairs of our own country before taking care of the entire world. There are many problems that need to be given priority such as social inequality, education, and health care.

Chapter 10:
Liberal Democracy

Introduction

Let us begin by asking the question, "Why are the majority of U.S. citizens and non-citizens apathetic?" Are people apathetic due to human nature, or is it due to social conditioning and as being the result of the political system? These are the questions this chapter will attempt to answer.[86]

On the one hand, there is a negative view of human nature – that humans are evil, selfish, individualistic, and apathetic. From this arises the need for a strong, centralized government to keep people under control. On the opposite spectrum is a positive view of human nature – that humans are by nature social beings, democratic, altruistic, and have great potential. Our social nature leads us to live and work together to achieve common goals, which results in having a democratic system where people deliberate to achieve something in the public sphere. This positive view of human nature can lead to statism to help citizens of a given society fulfill basic human necessities and to ensure that they are not exploited to enrich business. I will argue in favor of this latter position, and I will go further into detail about why we ought to have the appropriate political system to foster personal growth and the general advancement of human civilization. We are rational creatures. There is much more in life than merely pursuing base pleasures, economic and material wealth. We ought to pursue the things that we are capable of; we ought to strive for excellence. Doing so will lead to a more fulfilling and thus a happier life. I am in favor of the evolutionary process. Each generation should evolve to become better, instead of remaining static, and in the worst case scenario, regressing. To evolve is to understand and fulfill our human potential.

Let us begin my exploring the two contrasting views of human nature. This is important because it will enable us to understand the development of different political systems and its effects on the individual and society at large.

---

[86] The chapter was originally written under the supervision of Kenneth Peter, Political Science Professor and former Chair at San Jose State University. I am grateful for his support and guidance during my graduate years there.

Human Nature: The Underlying Foundation

The Negative View

On one side of the spectrum is the negative and pessimistic view of human nature. Humans are selfish and individualistic creatures who will primarily look after their own interests rather than those of others, which is why the majority of people in society are apathetic. An argument from biology is that we preserve ourselves and our relatives before others to ensure the survival of our gene pool.

Thomas Hobbes is a proponent of the negative view of human nature. The natural state (a state without government) is a state of war, where everyone is fighting everyone else to secure selfish interests. In order to increase our chances of survival, Hobbes argues that we must enter a social contract with a strong, centralized, impartial government, which has the supreme authority over society. This is the only way to protect the individual members within society and to ensure stability. The role of the state, therefore, is to constrain human behavior.

This negative view of human nature is also used by Joseph Schumpeter, by some of our founding fathers such as James Madison, and by similar thinkers to downplay democracy and deliberation. People are irrational and they are bound to get of control when they get together. For this reason, a republic is better, and deliberation and political power should be conducted by an elite class of qualified individuals. These people are often the most privileged within society. A certain amount of resources, education, and the right behavioral dispositions are required to achieve this status. The underlying philosophy of liberal democracy, the system that is in place today, is also based upon this view. Let us explore its psychological theory of human beings.

Liberal Psychology Based on the Negative View

Liberal psychology and liberal democracy approaches human nature from a negative perspective – that they are selfish and individualist.[87] We

---

[87] See Ch. 4: The Psychological Frame: Apolitical Man in Benjamin Barber, *Strong Democracy* (Berkley and Los Angeles: UC Press, 1984).

are alone is this world. "We are born in to the world as solitary strangers, live our lives as wary aliens, and die in fearful isolation."[88] The critic can argue that it is up to us to choose whether or not we want to live in solitude and be alienated from other people and from society. There are many people who would choose otherwise. Alienation is the paramount feature of liberal psychology. It is highly valued especially from the beginning in the Western tradition. We value individualism, we value solitude, we value our personal space, and we value our personal property. Certain social implications results from this view. Some of the implications are that men and women do not exist for each other, that there is no public good, there is no fraternal feelings, no general will, no mutuality, no species identity, and no "love or belief or commitment that is not wholly private."[89] We use other people as a means to an end, and that end is to fulfill our self interest.

Other psychological attributes of people is that they are hedonistic, aggressive, and acquisitive. People are hedonists because they pursue pleasure and their needs. They are aggressive because they want to obtain these interests and the power to do so. They are acquisitive because they have the desire to obtain personal property. People can be described as "need-driven, power-seeking, and property-acquiring." Power is a means to achieve our wants and needs. Power becomes an art of war. Under these conditions, politics "can only be the art or science of power – of who gets what, when, and how."[90] The realist fits perfectly into this picture. The realist also shares the view of liberal psychology. Since people are after their own interests, they must do what it takes to protect and to secure their personal interests, primarily their well-being including their survival. When we take this on to a larger scale, states are after their own interests, and since there is no sovereign power to oversee all the states within this world, it would be wise for each state to obtain as much power as possible to secure and protect its own interest. International politics is basically a politics of war involving multiple actors possessing different interests.

---

[88] Ibid. 68.

[89] Ibid. 72.

[90] Ibid.

Other important aspects of liberal psychology are variations with respect to the anarchist disposition, the realist disposition, and minimalist disposition. Let us first explore the meaning of these three dispositions. The anarchist disposition values privacy, liberty, individualism, property and rights. The realist disposition values the use of power, law, coercive mediation, and sovereign arbitration. The minimalist disposition values tolerance, wariness of government, pluralism, and the exercise of institutional caution to maintain a system of checks and balances. The American political system, as we will explore later on, possesses all three dispositions.

In the anarchist variation of liberal psychology, being an independent person is highly valued. Self-sufficiency implies independence and power. This implies being financially independent and psychologically independent and strong. Relying on others and being sociable is seen as a weakness. The individual with his or her small self can do great things. The pursuit of base needs can even lead to the conquest over nature and the mastering of its laws. The liberal variation is about people being unchallengeable. To the realist, efficiency is "an expression of rigidity and inflexibility. The politics resulting from this are limits, control, coercion, sanctions, and safeguards. The minimalist variation involves a mediating process and faith in prudential reasoning.

From this negative view of human nature, we can see that the political structure is used to limit human behavior. Nevertheless, liberal psychology states that we can achieve great things such as mastering the laws of nature. But this argument is narrow and limited. I will argue that there is a great deal more to human potential than achieving this. The structure of society resulting from the negative view of human nature ultimately inhibits our psychological and spiritual well-being. Let us now examine the positive side of human nature.

The Positive View

On the other end of the spectrum, humans are regarded as being social animals, possessing great intelligence, creativity and potential. Aristotle argues that the smallest unit within society is the family, the next level is the village, and the self-sufficient level is the city-state. The city-state is the most self-sufficient because people and institutions are in place to provide goods and services to everyone in the city. According to Aristotle, we cannot live a happy life until we have a self-sufficient life, and this self-sufficient life requires that we rely upon other people for goods and services that we cannot achieve by ourselves, which is the reason for the formation of the city-state.

Aristotle discusses a great deal more about human function and living the happy life in the *Nicomachean Ethics*. I will focus on his philosophy on human nature, that we are rational beings and that we ought to pursue excellence and a self-sufficient life so that we can live a happy life. What makes human beings stand out is our thinking faculty, which is higher than that of other animals. Another human trait that make us stand out is our curiosity to contemplate and try to solve various kinds of problems such as mathematical ones, ones dealing with the realm of physics, human behavior, the nature of the universe, and many others. We are also creative and spiritual beings, which can be seen in our pursuit of the arts such as music, drawing, painting, theatre, poetry, and the like. There is form as well as content in each one of these. Trying to understand and enhancing the form or the essence is our attempt towards perfection or excellence in these areas. It is then that we start to realize our own greatness. We do not merely pursue base pleasures and we do not merely look after our own interests. Human civilization would be quite boring and would not have advanced much if this were the case. First and foremost is our thinking faculty. Aristotle argues that we ought to use it to understanding our function and the things around us. We should use it to evolve.

Aristotle states that excellence is the mean between two extremes. There are two types of excellences. The first is moral excellence. The mean between two vices is the ideal. An example would be courage. The first vice is being a coward, and the other vice is being overly confident. Both vices can be detrimental and this is why we ought to aim for the mean, which is to be courageous. Achieving the mean is regarded as virtuous. What is virtuous is desirable because they are good for us. Intellectual excellence is the pursuit of theoretical as well as practical knowledge. Our knowledge of the world and the universe rests upon certain principles such as physical, biological, or mathematical ones. However, having theoretical knowledge is not enough. We must also find a use for it, otherwise it is a waste.

In addition to achieving these two forms of excellence to achieve a happy life, which Aristotle considers to be sufficient life, we must also pursue a social dimension. We are social animals. It gives us great pleasure to exercise our thinking faculty. It gives us great pleasure to contemplate on various issues, including political ones. It also gives us great pleasure in trying to solve problems, practical ones as well as theoretical ones. Examples of practical problems are those related to the public sphere, which is the intention of political deliberation. It brings us great pleasure when we are engaged in debates, such as those among our friends. Undergoing the deliberate process is exercising human rationality, which is a part of our function. This is the reason why people enjoy studying and debating issues when they are done in a critical manner, such as in the study of philosophy. Therefore, it is part of our natural function to socialize and debate with other people on an ongoing basis. The point is that we enjoy contemplating with others because it is enriching and brings us pleasures.

Human psychology also supports the view that we are social animals. We seek for attention, approval, love, and support from others. These needs create several levels of Abraham Maslow's hierarchy of needs. An overly rational person may deny these things in life after coming to the conclusion that to pursue these things is often irrational and requires a dependence upon other people. Furthermore, we must not let our passions enslave us, but rather they must be a slave to us. But to deny these things is to deny the essence of our own nature. We are passionate social beings, and to inhibit this side of us is leading to an incomplete and imbalanced psyche. Jung argues that we should be aware of our different archetypes and that we ought to get in touch with them otherwise there will be psychological neurosis leading to an unfulfilled and therefore an unhappy life. Jung, very much like Aristotle, argued that we need to have a balanced life. It is natural for us to seek a meaningful life, so much so that the media uses this to instill upon us superficial values such as conditioning us to associate with designer clothing because it will bring us status or conditioning us to live through lives of celebrities, as if we cannot define our own lives for ourselves. The psychologically and spiritually balanced life cannot be done based liberal psychology, and a society based on such a view is detrimental to human beings. Let us now explore the social and political implications resulting from these two views of human nature.

Liberal Democracy Resulting from the Negative View

Based upon the negative/pessimistic view of human nature, we get a society and political system that restrain human behavior due to the fear that people will cause chaos while pursing selfish interests. This view of human nature has a profound effect on nearly every important aspect of life. Let us explore these through the dispositions of liberal democracy.

Anarchist, Realist, and Minimalist Dispositions

The primary goal of liberal democracy is to promote liberty, advance interests, and to keep people safe from each other.[91] As a review, the anarchist disposition values privacy, liberty, individualism, and rights. The realist disposition values power, law, coercive mediation, and sovereign adjudication. The minimalist disposition values tolerance, wariness of government, pluralism, and the exercise of institutional caution to create a system of checks and balances. Once again, the American political system paradoxically possesses all three dispositions.

The anarchist disposition of liberal democracy is the apolitical element. The main thesis here is that as a result of a person's autonomy (which is the freedom from external constraint), the fulfillment of needs and wants can "(at least in the abstract) be satisfied outside of a coercive civil communities."[92] This implies that human beings are self-sufficient on their own, which goes directly against Aristotle's philosophy. A brief examination of this view makes it seem implausible because we often rely upon others within the community to have our basic needs and wants met, even with something as basic as food and water. According to the anarchist disposition and the notion of autonomy, problems arise from political participation rather than from non political participation. Human beings are not inherently political animals, and that the aim of the political

---

[91] Ibid. 4.

[92] Ibid. 6.

community is an instrument used to protect liberty, private interests, and chaos. And like Hobbes, citizenship is viewed as an artificial construct.

> Citizenship is an artificial role that the natural man prudently adopts in order to safeguard his solitary humanity. [W]e are political in order to safeguard ourselves as men...[93]

We can see why this view has significant implications for society. It leads to the hindrance of political participation and deliberation based on the thesis that it will create conflict. But this also means that people must be made to believe by whatever means necessary that politics in not important to their lives, and that they ought to leave it up to those who are more qualified. At the same time, they ought to be concerned about their own lives instead of others, and especially what is going on around the world since these matters do not concern the individual within this society.

The primary basis for the realist disposition in liberal democracy is the use of power as a means to an end. To keep people under control, a variety of methods are used including the use of fear, manipulation, enforcement, deterrence, and sanction. Realism in Western liberal democracy consists of legislatures and the courts deploying "penal sanction and juridical incentive aimed at controlling by manipulation – but not altering or transforming – hedonistic self-interest."[94] A good example of this is the American justice system. A large number of people are thrown in jail, but there are few rehabilitation programs. This, in essence, is like sweeping the problem under the rug rather than taking care of it. Since people are more concerned with selfish interests than that of the public, "people are not made to reformulate private interest in public terms but are encouraged to reformulate public goods in terms of private advantage."[95] People will analyze public goods and public policies in terms of their beneficiary values for themselves, and not that of the public. Therefore, when I go out to vote, I will vote if the proposition benefits me. I do not care whether it is beneficial to society at large. If matters of public policy do not affect me,

---

[93] Ibid. 8.

[94] Ibid. 13.

[95] Ibid.

then I have no interest in paying attention. From this, we get a lot of apathetic people - selfish individuals who are concerned with the advancement of their own interests and who fail to see the interconnectedness between their interests and that of the political and social system.

The politics of minimalism is the politics of toleration. The problem for the minimalist is on keeping the custodians under control. On the one hand, there ought to be a sovereign power to keep people under control, but on the other hand, this sovereign power might become too powerful and despotic. Power is necessary, but it must also be limited. The underlying principles rest on the attitudes of tolerance, skepticism, and wariness. Politics is seen "as relations among beings too dependent and too naturally competitive to live in peaceful solitude yet too distrustful to live easily in mutuality."[96] There is distrust of the individual, the majority, and of the state. It is therefore best to set up a system of checks and balances in government. It would also be better to have a representative democracy rather than direct democracy. When people come together to deliberate, they will only cause chaos. The collective power of the majority is authoritative, and is therefore dangerous. This is why the majority should be prevented from being a part of the political process. Fostering and maintaining the autonomy of different groups consisting of different interests is good under these circumstances.

Politics as Zoo Keeping and the Cost of Realism

Politics under the negative view of humans is a politics of zoo keeping. Manipulation of the people is a core component. The "liberal state manipulates men by first implanting terror in them and then, in return for their socially acceptable behavior and their prudential fealty, protecting them from it."[97] We can see this in the media and the government. They instill within us the fear of certain groups of people, such as Latinos and African Americans, because according the mainstream media, they conduct most of the crime and violence within society. The media also

---

[96] Ibid. 15.

[97] Ibid. 23.

tells us that society, in general is a dangerous place, therefore we need to be cautious and make sure that we have security systems for our homes and for our cars. One lock on the door does not seem to be enough. Some people have a total of four locks, two on the outer metal door, and two on the main door. Not only is society a dangerous place, the internet seems to be a dangerous place as well. It doesn't seem like we can get enough virus protection for our computer.

September 11, 2001 gave us a new fear – the fear of terrorists. The U.S. government uses this new threat to increase the Department of Defense spending, and the military industrial complex will benefit greatly from this. For example, DOD plans on procuring a new fleet of jet fighters called F-35 Joint Strike Fighter from Lockheed Martin Corporation. This family of fighters will be used in the Navy, Army, and Marine Corps. The Department of Defense (DOD) plans to procure a total of 2,443 F-35s, which will cost roughly $300 billion, between FY 2007 and FY 2035.[98] A total of 12 F-35s will be procured in FY 2008, totaling $2.6539 billion. In addition to the cost of procurement, another $3.4883 billion will be spent on research and development, for a combined total of $6.1422 billion for the F-35 Joint Strike Fighters in FY 2008.[99] On the grander scale, the total cost of national defense will be $647.2 billion in FY 2008, which includes a $141.7 billion requested for Global War on Terror (GWOT) operations, including military operations in Iraq and Afghanistan.[100] This is the real cost of realism, at the expense of tax payers. Tax payers are not only funding the national defense budget, which is 20% of the FY 2008 budget request, to protect us from the enemy, tax payers are also the ones funding the manipulation of the propaganda machine since the mainstream media

---

[98] Steven M. Kosiak, *Analysis of the FY 2008 Defense Budget Request* (Center for Strategic and Budgetary Assessments) 28. Publication is available at http://www.csbaonline.org/4Publications/PubLibrary/R.20070607.Analysis_of_th e_FY/R.20070607.Analysis_of_the_FY.pdf

[99] Steven M. Kosiak, *Historical and Projected Funding for Defense: Presentation of the FY 2008 Request in Tables and Charts* (Center for Strategic and Budgetary Assessments) Table 5. Publication is available at http://www.csbaonline.org/4Publications/PubLibrary/U.20070607.Historical_and_ Pro/U.20070607.Historical_and_Pro.pdf

[100] Ibid. Table 1.

gets their information from sources that include the White House and Pentagon.[101]

Walter Lippmann, a leading liberal democratic theorist, leading media figure, and part of the propaganda commission during the Wilson Administration, argues that that there two classes within society – the "specialized class" and the "bewildered herd". The "specialized class" is an elite group of "responsible men" that runs society and controls majority of the population or the "bewildered herd" from undermining their interests. Once again, people are viewed as untamed beasts, and they need to be kept under control, which is the purpose of the politics and the propaganda within the media.[102]

Other Psychological Dispositions

Liberal democracy also views the person as being small, static, inflexible, and one who cannot see beyond his or her own appetites. Neither can the liberal person bear the weight of his or her own ideals. This would imply that we should not be too idealist since we do not have the capacity to maintain and thus achieve our ideals. Upon examination of this view, it also seems implausible because it cannot account for some of the great accomplishments of human civilization, which often begins with some type of ideal, such as that of creating a just and efficient government whose primary goal is to take care of its people. We can indeed have ideals and these ideals can be achieved as long as they are realistic ideals that are within our power to achieve. And even if some of these ideals cannot be achieved, it does not mean that we should not have them. Having an ideal is having a sense of direction or a target to aim at. For this reason, Aristotle states that we should not live aimlessly. Freedom for the liberal person "becomes indistinguishable from selfishness and is corrupted from within by apathy, alienation, and anomie...."[103] Equality is market exchangeability, and happiness is "measured by material gratification to

---

[101] Noam Chomsky and Edward S. Herman, *Manufacturing Consent: The Political Economy of the Mass Media* (Pantheon Books, 2002).

[102] Noam Chomsky, *Media Control: The Spectacular Achievements of Propaganda*, 2nd ed. (New York: Seven Stories Press) 16.

[103] Barber, 24.

the detriment of the spirit."[104] Thus, liberal democracy goes hand in hand with our destructive and superficial consumer society.

Strong Democracy Resulting from the Positive View

The existing political system is liberal democracy, which is based on a negative view of human nature. In response to liberal democracy, Barber writes about having strong democracy, which is a political system that can accommodate and foster the positive and more optimistic philosophy of human nature. Strong democracy is more democratic, more egalitarian, and more just. It accommodates and fosters human rationality, deliberation, and the fact that we need to work together to achieve the common good, rather than to merely to pursue selfish interests such as profit making. In essence, strong democracy, even though one can argue that it is an ideal, is a more harmonious and thus a better system than liberal democracy, and for this reason, we should strive to achieve it.

What exactly is strong democracy? It is a self governing community where citizens are united by civic education. There is common purpose and mutual action, which are made possible "by virtue of [the citizen's] civic attitudes and participatory institutions rather than their altruism or their good nature."[105] Politics is seen not as a way of life, but rather as a way of living. Human beings can strive to live together to advance their mutual interests. Within strong democracy, there is a realm of "unique openness, flexibility, and promise."[106] Conflicts within this system are not merely dealt with, but are transformed "through a politics of distinctive inventiveness and discovery."[107]

---

[104] Ibid.

[105] Ibid. 117.

[106] Ibid. 119.

[107] Ibid.

The Conditions of Politics

What are the defining conditions of a good political system? Politics involves action, publicness, necessity, choice, reasonableness, conflict, and absence of an independent ground. The first condition of politics is that it involves participation and not observation, which is how a 'watchdog' or 'watchman' state would define it as being. It is meant for the citizens of a given society to participate in politics, and not merely be a spectator, which is exactly what the American political system is. The herd is called out once in a great while to participate, then they are encouraged to sit on the side lines once again to dwell in their superficial lifestyle and let the "specialized class" govern society. Participating in an activity is better than merely watching it because it is more enjoyable to carry out the activity rather than being passively exposed to it. The happy life according to Aristotle is an active life. We perform various activities and this often requires participating with other people. In this case, it is participating with others in the political sphere. The second condition of politics is that of publicness; politics has public consequences. Not all actions are political. It is only if it is intended to have public consequences that it is regarded as being political. The third condition is the necessity of carrying out action. "It is enmeshed in events that are part of a train of cause and effect already at work in the world."[108] Politics is therefore interdependent upon many variables within this world such as the economy and religion. In fact, economics is prior to politics in America. An interesting point Barber makes is that the choice of not making a decision also has public consequences. This is known as indecision. The fourth condition of politics is about choosing to do things and choosing among different options such as different political policies. But these choices must be made prudently and with careful consideration. "Action that is impulsive, arbitrary, or unconsidered is not yet political action."[109] This is where civic education comes into play. The fifth condition of politics is reasonableness. "A reasonable choice or a reasonable settlement is not necessarily rational at all, but it will be seen as deliberate, nonrandom,

---

[108] Ibid. 124.

[109] Ibid. 126.

uncoercive, and in a practical sense fair."[110] The sixth condition is that politics arise out of conflict:

> Formal consensus is sometimes described as 'agreeing to disagree,' but more accurate description would be 'agreeing on how to disagree': on whether, that is, to deal with conflict by suppressing it, ameliorating it, tolerating it, resolving it, or transforming it.[111]

Under the realist philosophy, power is used to overcome disagreement and conflict. Anyone disagreeing against U.S. policy or ideology is subject to the coercion of its power. A true democratic world would not allow this. The seventh condition is the absence of an independent ground. Since self-legislation and community-building are self-contained and self-correcting, they are "genuinely independent of external norms, prepolitical truths, or natural rights."[112]

Response to the Political Condition

Strong democracy is a response to the current political condition. The first response is about action. Citizens in strong democracy actively participate in the political process. Politics is done by, not to, citizens. "Activity is its chief virtue, and involvement, commitment, obligation, and service – common deliberation, common decision, and common work – are its hallmarks."[113] Liberal democracy on the other hand wants its citizens to stay out of politics and worry about their own personal affairs. But one's personal affairs is often interdependent with that of the public, therefore citizens ought to be politically active, rather than passive. The second response is the creation of a public that is capable in deliberation and decision making. Having a strong sense of community is important and is one of the chief tasks set forth by strong democracy. The third

---

[110] Ibid. 127.

[111] Ibid. 129.

[112] Ibid. 135.

[113] Ibid. 133.

response is the necessity of deliberation and decision making. Agency and responsibility are at the center of the political process. The fourth response is having the ability to choose. Conflict is transformed rather than being accommodated or limited. The fifth, reasonableness, the sixth, conflict, and the seventh, absence of independent ground has already been discussed. Political deliberation and decision must be made rationally, critically, carefully, without being haste. Self-legislation and community building occur independently of external norms. Strong democracy equalizes value inputs. Each participant is giving an equal opportunity to express his or her points of view.

I would like to go back and briefly discuss the coexistence of deliberation within democracy. In order to get things done, citizens in a strong democracy must engage in political deliberation – the coming together of a group of people to find a solution to solve a problem. Lynne M. Sanders argue that deliberation increases autonomy – that is, it increases the political awareness and participation of individuals instead of leaving it to a specialized group of people, or the more "responsible men". "Autonomy is a civic or political, not individualistic, project...."[114] The two prerequisites of deliberation are mutual respect and good oration skills. Citizens deliberating each other must address each other as equals, and must offer reasonable and justified arguments. Deliberators must be good orators, but some citizens are better than others. They must possess "epistemological authority," which is "the capacity to evoke acknowledgement of one's argument."[115] Another prerequisite of deliberation is to be able to have the resources to study public policy and to deliberate, such as time, money, and education. Deliberation in America is neither truly deliberative nor democratic. Material prerequisites are unequally distributed. Some Americans are more persuasive than others, and some are less listened to than others (such as people of more prestigious backgrounds). Mutual respect is practically remote. In order to improve the conditions for deliberation, citizen respect must be

---

[114] Lynne M. Sanders, "Against Deliberation", *Political Theory* v 25 (3) (June, 1997): 347 – 376.

[115] Ibid. 349.

heightened, there must be formalization of equal access, and there must be structural and economic reform.

Citizenship

One of two other important dimensions of strong democracy is citizenship. The other is community. Let us focus upon the former first. There must be civic bond among its citizens for a society to be a strong, harmonious, and functioning civil society. Aristotle states that it is this civic bond that orders and governs all other types of bonds. It is "the bond that creates the public structure within which other, more personal and private social relationships can flourish."[116] The civic bond is an inevitable result of mutual interests especially the basic and necessary conditions of life – food, shelter, security, and love. Civic bond is required to have a functioning civil society.

What are the qualifying conditions of citizenship? To help us to understand, let us examine Barber's classification of the three types of political systems and their corresponding style of citizenship. Let us first explore the three types of democratic systems and then the character and quality of civic bond in each type of system. The first is representative democracy. Citizens in this type of political system are conceived as legal entities and are bound together by a social contract, very much like philosophy of Hobbes. The political style is distrustful and passive because people are selfish individuals looking after their own interests and are not concerned with a greater good. The second political system is unitary democracy. In this political system, citizens conceive each other as brothers and are bound metaphorically by blood. We are united because we are of the same kind. The political style is self-abnegating [a giving up psychology] and people are submissive. The third political style is strong democracy. In this system, citizens are conceived as neighbors and they are bound together by common participatory activity. The political style involves cooperation and carrying out political activity. Let us now explore the character and quality of civic bond in each type of political system. Let us keep in mind that the way people behave in society is due to the structure of the political system, which was created based on a corresponding view of human nature.

---

[116] Barber, 217.

In representative democracy, citizens are related to the government as sovereign individuals, but they are also subjects to the sovereign power, which is there to protect and unite its citizens. According to Hobbes, we enter a social contract with a sovereign and supreme power because we need it to protect us against ourselves. People are naturally selfish and evil, and we will do whatever it takes to secure our life, liberty, needs, and wants. The natural state is a state of war. The sovereign power acts as an impartial judge to handle disputes and uphold the law by force in order to achieve a civil society. Contracts must be enforced otherwise people will not carry them out. Civic ties in a representative democracy are with the government only and relations with others are private. In other words, the most important civic relation we have is directly with the government because it protects and provides us with the primary necessities of life. Our relationship with other people is minimal according to this system. The civic virtue in this system is based on accountability, or what Barber calls reciprocal control. We must hold the government accountable for its action to protect our interest. To achieve accountability, there ought to be transparency, a fundamental characteristic of democracy. There also ought to be a system of checks and balances to keep the governmental structures from abusing its own powers. Accountability is also reciprocal. The state must holds its citizens accountable by making sure that every citizen upholds the law and does not undermine the sovereignty and function of the state. This is valid only if the state carries out its original function and if it does so well, otherwise one can argue that it is the right of the citizens to undermine its sovereignty.

In unitary democracy, citizens are related to the government as a corporate body. The state is the CEO, and everyone else is an employee of the company. All employees must obey management and carry out the assigned work. What is our assigned task in this country? It is to work and to give a share of our money away to the pubic treasury so that the government can provide its people with public goods and services. Of course, it often becomes abusive such as in the case of this government. An average of four hundred billion dollars was spent on the military alone prior to 2001. In the fiscal year of 2008, $647.2 billion is requested for national defense, making up 20% of the total federal budget request for that year. This is based on a realist view of politics – international relationships is a state of war, therefore the U.S. government must do what it takes to remain the supreme power, which means that it has to make sure that no one surpasses or comes close to its military might. In this world, the driving ethical theory is that might makes right. Civic virtue in unitary democracy is based on fraternity – love and fear are reciprocal. We love our government as if it were our parents because it sets the conditions that enable us to carry our lives. We also fear the government because of its domination over us. It can punish and take away our rights when deemed necessary. The government loves its citizens when they are behaving properly, like when children behave properly towards their parents. The government is also fearful of its citizens because they can act with retaliation, just like children can retaliate against their parents.

In strong democracy, citizens are related to the government as active participants. Citizens take an active role in local, state, and national governance because of shared mutual interests. The purpose of the state is to govern society. The rules, regulations, and laws affect my life, which is why it is within my interest to keep abreast of the political situation and to participate in the political process. People often fail to realize the extent public policy, especially significant ones such as the choice to go to war, has on our lives, culture, and the rest of society. The civic virtue in strong democracy is civility. There is reciprocal empathy and respect.

The American idea of citizenship incorporates all three civic formulas:

> A contractual element informs the legal conception of citizenship (the American as a person at law); a communal element lies behind the national conception of citizenship (the American as a native-born Yankee); and an activist element supports the civic conception of a citizenship used in devising standards for 'new' citizens (The America as a literate, participating actor).[117]

Based on these conflicting values, it is no wonder that our society has a difficult time achieving justice (in the harmonious sense). Our original intentions ought to be clear in order for us to move forward. This is why we ought to examine our political system at its historical roots. We ought to iron out inconsistencies, problems, and other variables that inhibits society and its people from achieving our full human potential by

---

[117] Ibid. 228.

deconstructing every component, very much the same way Immanuel Kant meticulously deconstructed the foundations of knowledge, ultimately deriving the conditions that makes for the possibility of knowledge itself. Let us now explore another important aspect of strong democracy – having a strong sense of community.

Strong Democratic Community

Here, Barber also brings up three types of community and each corresponding characteristics. The reason for doing so is to deduce that having a strong democratic community is the best for society. The first is the individualist community. The value associated with this community is that people are selfish individuals who look after their own interests. Barbers states that this argument commits a fallacy because it presupposes that a "community represents only the characteristics of its constitutional parts."[118] The community is more than just the sum of its parts. A community has emergent properties such as the mind is an emergent property of the brain. A community is the result of a multitude of variables including its people, its institutions, and a plurality of values and norms. These components do not exist independently of each other. They each participate in a dynamic that creates a sense of community. The other extreme view is that of the organic community, in which the individual is sublimated into the organic whole. The problem with this view is the opposite of the first. It is held that the community is not a result of its constituent parts, which is of course not true. The third type of community, and one that Barber argues in favor of, is strong democratic community (in strong democracy). Unlike the other two, individuals in this type of community are transformed through there interaction and common interests with one another. I am in favor of this form as well because it supports my argument that we are social animals, and that we should fulfill our human potential. The evolutionary growth of individuals will inevitably lead to the growth of society, because the individuals are the constituent parts of a given society. We will exert our values onto the structure of society so that it enables us to carry out and fulfill what it is that we value. If I value human growth, then I would want a system that will foster and enable the growth of every individual living under that

---

[118] Ibid. 231.

society. What causes transformation in strong democratic community? It is the result of having to work together to achieve mutual interests. By working together, we must share, criticize, and debate each other's suggestions on achieving a certain goal. Finding the best and most efficient solution will naturally result from this process. We must also learn how to be harmonious because we must be able to work with each other if we want to accomplish the task.

The Facilitating Conditions of Citizenship in Strong Democracy

There are three primary factors needed to facilitate a strong democratic community: civic education, leadership, and morals and values. Civic education takes on three forms. The first is formal pedagogy, involving the teaching of civics, history, and citizenship. We already have this in place, but students ought to be exposed using a more critical approach. Mainstream textbooks are often one sided and used to promote the mainstream ideology. Students should be exposed to both sides of the issue. Teachers should use a pedagogy that actively engages students in the learning process rather than treating them as passive receptacles of knowledge. One good way is to use the dialectic method, which is often used in philosophy. Civic education should also expose people to the complete picture. It currently does not because the information provided in academia, just like the media, is manipulated so that people will believe in certain things that will make them be more passive citizens, so that they will support the system and those in control, and to stay out of the way of those benefiting the most from the current social and political structure. It is obvious that powerful and influential individuals and corporations would want to minimize people would undermine their interests. Economic interest is perhaps the primary one. To provide such an education will likely cause friction among the citizens and those who are in control, and this is something that the latter does not want. Classroom education is of course not enough. There has to be hands on experience to reinforce what we learn in the classroom. In fact, learning from the real world is more important than learning from a textbook because we can experience and not merely read about the course material. This is why there ought to be private-sphere social activity. Participating in local politics is a good and a convenient ground for civic education. The third form is participatory politics. A truly civic education must involve activities that bring public consequences.

The second facilitating condition of citizenship according to Barber is leadership. He makes an interesting argument about how in representative systems, there are only leaders and followers. The majority of people within society are merely followers of the system. I believe this is an inaccurate statement. Within our own society, there are indeed many passive followers and few leaders. But there are also many people out there who are trying to create positive change. These people are not merely followers nor or they the true leaders (the ones that are in control of system). They are, however, leaders in the local sense. Barber argues that there are no leaders in the ideal political system. "Complete self-government by an active citizenry would leave no room for leaders or follows."[119] I, however, will argue that there is bound to be a certain degree of leaders and followers even within the ideal system because there will still be a hierarchy of sorts, therefore there will still be people giving orders to others to follow. We cannot have a true egalitarian society, as Aristotle would argue. Children cannot be truly equal to their parents, and employees cannot be equal to their employers. Barber's real argument here seams to be that in the ideal system where citizens engage in the day-to-day affairs of society, governance takes on a decentralized form, consisting of bottom-up management, and horizontal rather than vertical management. All of this is due to the many parties being engaged in the process instead of having just a few dictating from the top.

The third facilitating condition of citizenship is having the appropriate morals and values among citizens to enable strong democracy:

> Without loyalty, fraternity, patriotism, neighborliness, bonding, tradition, mutual affection, and common belief, participatory democracy is reduced to class proceduralism; it becomes hardly less mechanistic than the self-interested contractualism of the liberal state it purports to supplant.[120]

Democracy by its nature requires tolerance, working together, and a strong civic bond in order to get the job done. These, like any other behavioral

---

[119] Ibid. 238.

[120] Ibid. 242.

dispositions, ought to be fostered among the young and through their education.

The Limiting Conditions of Citizenship

There are two major factors that limit the conditions of citizenship. The first is the problem of scale. We have a representative democracy because there are just too many people to come together under one roof to govern society. The criticism against having a representative democracy instead of a direct democracy is that it dissociates the majority of the people from politics because the system does not allow much room for political participation. We have a small group of people dictating policies for over 300 million people. Rousseau argued that representation alienates the politicians from the people and the people from the politicians. Politicians cannot make the best decision if they do not have a firsthand account of the local condition. The center is dissociated from the peripheral, which is why governance is best on a smaller scale.

John S. Dryzek offers several solutions to the problem of scale.[121] The first is to restrict political participation to a small number of occasions. People ought to deliberate and vote on issues and policies that will have profound effect on society, such as whether or not a country should go to war. He also suggests that we select representatives either by popular election or by random selection. If the latter, society is responsible to make sure that each citizen has the education to become a good representative. The third suggestion is for representatives to make decisions that take into consideration the interest of those who cannot participate in the political process. This process is called *internal-individuation*. The other factors to take into consideration are the future generations and the nonhuman world. This process is called factoring in the community of the affected.

Technological advancements and institutional improvements can also help to rectify the problem of scale. People can see live political deliberation among their representatives in their own living room via the television or the Internet. With modern forms of communication, it is possible for people to participate in the political decision process by

---

[121] John S. Dryzek, "Legitimacy and Economy in Deliberative Democracy", *Political Theory* 29 (5) (October, 2001): 651 – 669.

casting votes either through the telephone or through the Internet, which takes merely seconds to achieve. Technological advancements makes it possible for people to realize what is going on in nearly every corner of the world and it allows people to unite with other people around the planet. Ignorance and lack of communication is therefore not a good excuse.

The second problem is inequality, argued as being the result of capitalism. The argument made by Milton Friedman is that democracy is inseparable from capitalism. It is argued that in a free-market system, competition and greater incentives will result in innovation, creativity, and better and cheaper goods and services for consumers. Businesses are held accountable by the shareholders and by the rest of the community. Therefore, businesses must operate according to the appropriate norms, and there must be transparency to allow the public to see the inner operations of the business. Consumers will naturally favor certain business over others. In a similar spirit, citizens will favor certain political candidates over others, such as those who have the interests of the people in mind, rather than those who want the reign of power to advance personal interests. The first criticism against capitalism is that politics ought to precede economics, and not the other way around:

> If we wish to make central values as freedom and equality the measure of democracy, then we must regard them as the products rather than the conditions of the political process – which is to say that politics precedes economics and therefore creates the central values of economy and society.[122]

The underlying philosophy of capitalism is competition and profit making. It is not about striving for equality, justice, or achieving human potential. Politics in this country is ruled by these economic interests. Natural or human made destruction is coined in economic terms. Achieving economic success is seen as the main virtue. Capitalism is an efficient system, but mainly in economic terms. Economics is prior to politics in this country because public policy is influenced by money such as campaign contributions from wealthy individuals or corporations. Another criticism is that privatization is a threat. The interests of private actors can undermine private rights and values. The purpose of business is to make a

---

[122] Ibid. 252.

profit, which can include subverting the market itself by creating monopolies to advance personal interests. This is an empirical fact. Politics is tied into business. Major corporations line the pockets of politicians so that politicians can allow for the existence of monopolies. Friedman might respond by saying that this is not the true free-market at work. It is rather a result of human greed and selfishness, which is why I argue that the state must intervene to keep these things from happening in order to do what is best for society. We cannot have pure capitalism if we want to promote things such as equality, justice, and other fundamental human rights, and thus it would be more appropriate to have a hybrid economic system such as socialism.

Conclusion

Liberal democracy is a result of a negative view of human nature. Strong democracy is a result of the positive view of human nature. I argue for the latter. The unique aspect about human beings is our high capacity to reason, which enables us to ponder a variety of questions such as of our own existence and the nature of everything around us. Unlike other animals, we have the creative capacity to create works of art, music, poetry, and the like. We also have the ability to strive towards human excellence and strive to achieve our human potential. We have the amazing ability to come up with complex theories and explore the micro-universe and macro-universe. All of these characteristics are indeed an accurate description of human beings. The issue of whether we are naturally good or evil is a complicated one. Both sides have good arguments. We are greedy creatures, which can be used in a bad way, to pursue selfish interests that do not concern others. On the other hand, we can use this greed to pursue a greater good to increase social utility. Not only do we want to improve ourselves, we want others to improve as well.

Why do we have a negative view of human nature in modernity, and why did the classical age have a positive view? My argument is that the Greeks had a genuine interest in pursuit of human excellence through reason, which corresponds to philosophers such as Aristotle and Plato. This is not the case in the modern age. A negative view of human nature results in the creation of a social and political system that does not benefit the majority, but mainly the minority. The minority is out to primarily advance their own interests including the pursuit of economic wealth and the power of coercion. The negative view of human nature goes hand in hand with capitalism. People are selfish, individualistic, apathetic, and are not concerned with achieving human potential. Economic success is a factor in happiness, but it should not be the dominant one.

Part III: Economy and State Intervention

Why do some states adopt the free market economy, while others adopt the command economy? What are the benefits and drawbacks of each? The underlying principles of the free market economy are a market driven by the invisible hand, competition, which leads to innovation, higher quality goods and services, and lower prices. The market will work itself through the survival of the fittest and through the natural law of supply and demand. For these reasons, proponents of the free market argue that government should not intervene. Critics of the free market argue that the free market economy is a big playing ground for selfish individuals and corporations. Greed for profit can lead to a variety of negative consequences such an anti-democratic monopolies and the underpinning of justice and rights. A good case study of this is the former Enron in which selfish individuals associated with Enron (intellectuals and lawyers at Harvard University, and board members of various banks including those on the board of directors at Enron) working together since the early 1990's to deregulate the energy market. In the end, this group was responsible for the brief monopolization of energy in the United States and the eventual collapse of Enron. This is the ultimate fear of what the free market allows.

On the opposite spectrum are the proponents of the command economy, otherwise known as communism. The underlying principle of the command economy is for the government to take care of its people. This is done through state owned industries, direct intervention in the market to control supplies and prices, and providing various social programs to the population such as free health care, education, subsidized housing, and even subsidized groceries. The underlying philosophy of such a system is in essence for the state to provide its populace with the basics necessities to thrive in life. Discrepancies in income and social classes will lead to conflict. This sounds like a great utopia. However, reality has shown that the implementation of such ideals by the state has led to a variety of negative consequences. In order to provide social programs, the state needs a source of revenue, such as income taxes, business taxes, or revenue from state owned agencies. Countries that often adopt this form of economy are oftentimes extremely poor. For this reason, the states of command economy often print money to cover expenses, which leads to hyper inflation or the de-valuation of the local currency, driving people into greater poverty and inequality. A lack of competition due to state owned industries leads to a lack of incentive for innovation and higher quality goods and services. What is the point of creating better products if the state is going to pay people their salaries regardless? Such state owned industries often operate in the red, that is, they are not making a profit, but are nevertheless kept afloat to maintain employment. A lack of employment leads to social unrest, and social unrest can lead to political unrest. This is something that governments would want to avoid. Too much bureaucracy (often referred to as red tape) also prevents businesses from getting things done in a timely manner. These are the reasons why the command economy has not thrived compared to its free market counterpart. These are also the reasons that led many countries such as Vietnam, the case study of the next chapter, and China to adopt the free market economy during the 1980's and 1990's. Countries such as Vietnam and China realized that they must adopt the standard economic system or at least a hybrid version in order to prosper.

Chapter 11:
Economic Liberalization in Vietnam

Introduction

The government of Vietnam decided to undergo decentralization and economic liberalization in 1986 when the country faced major economic and social problems including hyper inflation and food shortages. The country has slowly been undergoing decentralization and market liberalization for the past twenty years, and major developments can be seen since. The purpose of this chapter is to explore these developments to help us better understand the effects of economic liberalization, in other words, to understand the effects of the free market system. I will also argue that the Communist Party of Vietnam (CPV) should learn from Venezuela (discussed in the next chapter) so that they can gain a strong foundation of popular support if they want to remain in power. The VCP should ensure that basic necessities of the people such as food, housing, utilities, healthcare, and education are met. Once these are met, society will be more harmonious and people can concentrate on developing their skills to enter the work force. In return, the VCP will gain the people's support in the future. Let us now begin by examining Vietnam's economic development.

Economic Development

GDP and Trade

Since the decision to decentralize and liberalize, the economy of Vietnam has shown tremendous growth. GDP doubled from 1991 – 2000.[123] GDP grew by 7.5% each year over the last five years, and 8.5% in 2005. Each year, 1.4 million people are entering the labor market.[124] The same source cited that the private sector is the most efficient in creating new and sustainable jobs. A major problem Vietnam faces is the widening gap between the rich and the poor even though GDP per family has increased from US $580 in 2004 to US $640 in 2005. This is partly the

---

[123] VietNamNet, news available at http://www.vietnam.net

[124] Vietnam Development Gateway, available at http://www.vietnamgateway.org

result of low foreign investment in undeveloped regions. But the government already has a program aimed at developing these poor regions. We will examine this further when we explore Vietnam's social achievements of Doi Moi, or the New Era.

In 2003, wage reforms were carried out to stimulate the economy and also to preserve political and social security.[125] The new wage is based on labor productivity and the country's income and economic growth. Wage reform is beneficial in three ways. It should help to create a healthy market, attract more qualified workers to work for the State, and increase the ethics of factory and public employees.

The country has also undergone a tremendous growth in bilateral trade. The Ministry of Finance reports that 86 agreements have been signed on bilateral trade and 47 others have been signed on investment protection.[126] Vietnam has established trade relations with 224 countries and territories.[127] Over 160 countries, including the EU, United States and Canada, now possess goods and services from Vietnam.[128] Major exports include crude oil, rice, aquatic products, coffee, rubber, and garments. The export level for December, 2005 is expected to reach US $3 billion, and the total for the calendar year is US $32 billion. The five largest export markets are the US ($4.8 billion), ASEAN ($4.4 billion), the EU ($4.3 billion), Japan ($3.5 billion), and China ($2.3 billion). The number of exporters has now reached 35,714, "an increase of 965 times compared to 1986."[129]

---

[125] VietNamNet, 10-23-2003

[126] Vietnam Ministry of Finance, news available at http://www.mof.gov.vn

[127] Business-Vietnam Open Markets, news available at http://www.bvom.com on 12-06-2005

[128] Vietnam Ministry of Finance

[129] Business-Vietnam Open Markets, 12-06-2005

Investment Capital

A major source of funding for social and economic development comes from foreign investment capital. The benefits of foreign investments are the following:

> It is a key factor in generating more employment and high-value products, enhancing management capability, fostering export markets and facilitating Vietnam's efforts to join the world economy.[130]

Foreign investment makes up almost 30% of the total social investment capital and provides employment for hundreds of thousands for people. The two major funds are the Official Development Assistance (ODA) fund and the Foreign Direct Investment (FDI) fund. The ODA fund makes up 5% of net investment capital and totaled US $28.78 billion between 1993 and 2004. A record amount of US $3.4 billion was raised in 2005 in the ODA fund. The total investment capital for the last 11 months is US $5.3 billion, an increase of 40.3% from the same period last year. International donors have already pledged US $3.7 billion for 2006 to help Vietnam reduce poverty and stimulate economic growth, under the condition that Hanoi will attempt to improve its governance and fight corruption. Japan is the largest single donor (US $835 million) followed by the EU (US $936 million).

In the next five years, Vietnam needs around US $140 billion to continue to develop the country. "Investment capital is expected to increase from 37.5% to 40%, while capital from the private sector may rise from 25% to 24%."[131] Another source of capital will come from the issuance of government bonds, construction bonds, and corporate bonds.

A major problem that needs to be addressed is that these sources are poured in low-value economic sectors. For this reason, it will not have a major impact on the growth of the economy.[132] It has been suggested that the government needs to focus on attracting more foreign investment. In

---

[130] Ibid.

[131] Ibid. on 12-07-05

[132] Vietnam Ministry of Finance, 12-12-2005

order to make Vietnam more appealing, "the country should improve the role of scientific and technological application."[133] Businesses need to reduce production and other costs and be more competitive. The same source also suggested the need for more investment in the private sector because it generates more money than the foreign-invested sector:

> According to Dr. Doanh [senior economist from the Prime Minister Research Commission], Vietnam's economy may gain a growth rate of at least nine per cent if a focus is given to the private sector, which has capital volume double that of the foreign-invested sector and has generated more jobs for local people.[134]

The same suggestion has also been made about Venezuela. In order to achieve long-term prosperity, a country needs to invest in its domestic businesses. This ensures that more money will stay within the country, which is a major criticism made by Hugo Chavez against foreign businesses.

Thirty-eight to 40% of GDP will go toward development in the next five years. Money will be spent on education, training, science, and technology. Education appears to be receiving the biggest share. It will account for 20% of the state budget. ODA capital will go into the development of the social-economic infrastructure. It will also be used to tackle social, environmental, and educational problems.

Reducing State-owned Enterprises (SOE)

State-owned enterprises (SOEs) are crucial elements of the VCP. Vietnam's policy is to maintain full ownership of industries that ensure public security and national defense. For other SOEs, the government will attract foreign investment to make them thrive. Vietnam has reduced its state-owned enterprises in order to meet economic growth target. The goal is to raise growth from 7% to 8% a year. There are currently fewer than 3,200 SOEs from more than 5,600 in 2001, but those that are still under state control are the ones that bring in the most revenue.

---

[133] Ibid.

[134] Ibid.

The problem with SOEs is that they are unproductive, they drain government resources, and they hinder growth. This has resulted in the banking system having to face high levels of debts from the loans made to these SOEs. They are kept afloat because they provide employment for a lot of people, just like in the case with China. A high level of unemployment is likely to cause social unrest, and the ruling party fears that they will lose popular support as a result of this. Let us now explore the social achievements of Doi Moi starting with poverty reduction.

Social Development

One of the greatest social achievements of Doi Moi is poverty reduction in Vietnam. The poverty level was at 70% in the mid-1980s and fell to 58% by 1993. By 1998, the poverty level was estimated to be at 37%.[135] According to the CIA Fact Book, poverty rate is estimated at 19.5% during 2004.[136] A very successful program is the government's Programme 135, which is implemented in 2,410 communes of 330 districts in 52 provinces.[137] The program has reduced poverty-stricken households by 40% since 1998, and each year, it is able to reduce the number of poor households by 4 to 5 percent. Ninety-six percent of highland residents receive medical checkups throughout 390 hospitals and clinics. In addition to providing health care, the Programme 135 also focuses on other infrastructure development such as electricity, roads, and schools. Over 20,000 other projects have been initiated resulting in the construction of over 6,500 roads and bridges and allowing 97% of poor communes with motor vehicle access. Sixty-four percent of highland households have access to electricity and 70% have access to clean water. Programme 135 also led to the development of more than 5,000 schools and classrooms, which provide access to 90% of minority children. Social developments in Vietnam also suggest that people are more valuable than the pursuit of profit. An example of this is at Cho Ray, the largest hospital in Ho Chi

---

[135] Vietnam Development Gateway, 10-24-2005

[136] CIA Fact Book at http://www.cia.gov/library/publications/the-world-factbook/geos/vm.html#Econ

[137] Vietnam Development Gateway, 10-24-2005

Minh City. Patients are allowed to pay for their treatments at a later date, instead of the conventional up-front policy adopted elsewhere. Payments can also be made in interest-free installments. Let us now explore the developments made in education.

Another great achievement of Vietnam's Doi Moi is in literacy and education. Ninety-four percent of adults are literate.[138] Net enrollment rate for school is 92% for primary and 74% for secondary schools. There has been an increase in the enrollment of ethnic minorities, partly due to the construction of schools in more convenient locations. Children of poor families receive fee exemptions and other incentives. The number of students studying abroad has increased, and so has the number of private and semi-private schools.

The education system of Vietnam possesses many problems despite the high literacy rate and increase in school enrollment. Attendance and completion rates are unsatisfactory. The quality of education is poor and poor staffing is a problem. The traditional style of learning is rote memorization, and there is little opportunity for creativity and expression of ideas. This creates a passive learning environment where they will not fully benefit from the learning process. Instead, they ought to be engaged in an active learning process. One such process is the use of the dialectic method, or the question and answer method, which enables students to critically reflect upon the issue. Knowledge of specialized curriculum, information technology, foreign languages and overall professional skills are poor among the staff. Training programs, equipment, teaching aids and textbooks are outdated. Significant topics such as ethics, lifestyle, and career guidance are also not adopted into the curriculum. The quality of education is undermined by the overemphasis on obtaining qualification, and this will have a negative long-term effect on citizens comprising every aspect of society. These shortcomings are attributed to a variety of factors including the sluggish pace of reform, poor administration, and rapid demand outpacing supply.

The goals to improve the educational system are as follows. The government should help students pursue a higher education by enabling them to first attend intermediate school. Schools should have a more effective style of instruction – one that fosters creativity and thinking, and not just mere rote memorization. Hi-level vocational training should also

---

[138] Ibid. 7-25-2003

be offered, but before this can happen, faculty members themselves must be educated so that they can be up to par with the market trends, especially in information technology. There must also be an improvement in educational management. Eighteen percent of the state budget is scheduled to be set aside for education next year, and this number will increase to 20% by 2010. Money should be set aside for scholarships to attract students, and teachers should be offered a generous salary to help retain current ones and attract new ones. There ought to be harsher enforcement for cheating to help maintain and increase the reputation and value of obtaining a degree.

Vietnam has shown a lot of social and economic improvement ever since the VCP decided to adopt decentralization and economic liberalization, but the VCP faces the dilemma of doing so while maintaining political control. This is where they can learn from some of the policies adopted by Hugo Chavez in the Venezuelan Revolution. Maintaining political control will require popular support. Let us now examine how Chavez is able to do this.

Learning from Venezuela

There is a key distinction from Vietnam and Venezuela. The revenue of Vietnam comes from state owned enterprises, taxes, and from foreign donations. Venezuela on the other hand extracts its wealth from its domestic oil reserves. This is how Venezuela is able to provide its citizens with many social benefits while defying U.S. policy, IMF policy, and other major international players in the global capitalist system, which is seen as a threat by Chavez and also by the VCP. VCP on the other hand must slowly merge with the global economy in order to develop the country because they cannot afford the same luxury of being an independent country like Venezuela can.

Venezuela adopts the Bolivarian Alternative for Latin America and the Caribbean (ALBA) instead of Free Trade Area of the Americas (FTAA). The latter is seen as detrimental towards social justice and equality. Venezuela's critique of FTAA mirrors their constitution. It emphasizes that there ought to be more equality between countries. There also ought to be national sovereignty and that the state should develop and create jobs for its people. The people have a right to free education, healthcare, and food security. This means respectively that there ought to be no privatization, no corporate patent rights, and no bio-piracy. Venezuela provides these basic rights through what are called "missions" as discussed in the next chapter:

1. Mission Ribas provides free high school education, which includes food, accommodation and travel expenses. On June 1, 2005, 20,686 people have graduated from these schools. Chavez has decided to increase the budget for Mission Ribas by $50 million per month.

2. Mission Sucre provides free college education. By the end of 2005, 210,000 people graduate from college.

3. Mission Barrior Adentro provides free healthcare to the people of Venezuela. It is supported by more than 20,000 Cuban doctors. The reason why Cuban doctors are brought in is because there is a lack of Venezuelan doctors to meet the needs of patients. This mission resulted in over 184 million consultations and saved more than 25,000 lives.

4. Mission Mercal subsidized supermarkets to make food more affordable for the general populace. Over 25,000 of these supermarkets exist and they capture 60% of the overall food market. They sell food up to 50% cheaper than private, capitalist chains. Mission Mercal was prompted by the 2002 – 2003 oil strike, which resulted in severe shortage of food and other basic necessities. The program has been boosted by $295 million of additional funding to expand existing outlets and to create another 1,000 food houses to provide for the very poor.

The VCP should adopt similar state welfare policies to maintain and increase popular support because the people will be happy if their basic necessities and rights are met, especially food and healthcare. If money is a problem, then the VCP should see it as an investment into the social system and in the party's future, therefore they should do whatever it takes to provide these things to the people. The primary purpose of any government is to ensure the safety and security of its people, otherwise there will be social unrest and it undermines the sovereignty and validity of the government.

Since Vietnam is about to emerge into the global economy, the VCP will need to adopt policies that will retain the country's sovereignty, security, and the party's political rule. In the case of Vietnam, excluding privatization is not an option. What they can do is learn from Venezuela. For private banks and other major corporations, the VCP can adopt a policy to implement state representatives on the board of directors of each of these companies so ensure that business policy is kept in line with the interests of the government. And like Venezuela, it would also help to have workers to be on the board of the directors or at least have a say in the internal policy making of these companies. In order to increase legitimacy, the government must provide transparency in its operations and also take responsibility for its mistakes. Doing so will help gain popular support, both domestic and abroad. At the same time, the VCP should continue to keep certain sectors under state control, primarily those that will ensure sovereignty and those that are essential to the basic necessities and rights of the people such as utilities and education. In order to be a global competitor, Vietnam will have to be up to par with international businesses. One way to help them achieve this is to welcome foreign companies to use its domestic cheap labor. In return, Vietnam, like China, will learn the skills and technologies and the manufacturing of goods for these foreign companies. Once Vietnam acquires this knowledge, foreign companies should be forced out, and Vietnam should continue to manufacture the same goods and profit from them by selling it directly to domestic and foreign markets. Vietnam should learn from Venezuela, China, and others to ensure its sovereignty and long-term interests. The government must also catch up and try to stay ahead of the game if they want its country to be competitive in the global market.

Conclusion

Vietnam, like many other Asian countries, possesses a determined and strong workforce. The government needs to adopt the appropriate policies to advance the country into the new century. It also needs to crack down on corruption and it needs to increase efficiency. If the government is corrupt, then other areas of society will not be efficient as well. The VCP must maintain popular support if they want to stay in power. To do so, it must ensure that its people have access to basic necessities and rights such as food, housing, employment, and education. But a society will not progress if its citizens are not creative, insightful, and educated. For this reason, education must be reformed in order to meet these needs. It is within the long-term interest of society to do so. If the VCP and Vietnam want to set an example for others, the government must find ways of adopting both economic liberalization and state welfare to improve its economic system, but at the same time provide the essential rights and necessities to its people. And unlike the West, Vietnam should also be careful not to allow profit and greed (economics) to precede the role of the government in providing for the safety and security of the people (politics). To do so will hopefully create a more harmonious society than that of the West. If successful, Vietnam will be a role model for other socialist countries to follow.

Chapter 12:
Venezuela and State Welfare

Introduction

Venezuela is a heap of trouble according to Western imperial powers such as the U.S. Government, the IMF, the World Bank, and other pro-capitalists. Venezuela is in favor of a command economy and actually cares about the rights of people to receive free healthcare, education, and other basic necessities that allow people to live decent lives. Perhaps most striking of all is its stance against the U.S. government and the international capital market. Venezuela defies IMF policy and adopts their own because they believe that it is wrong to exploit human labor in the name of profit. They also set up an allegiance in the region to gain political support, but at the same time helping out more poor and disadvantage countries.

The purpose of this chapter is to analyze the social and economic achievements of Venezuela to help us understand why such a country uses state welfare to increase social utility instead of operating on a pure free market philosophy to maximize economic efficiency. Doing so will hopefully make the reader more optimistic about alternative styles of governments and economies. I will also argue that Venezuela should develop a hybrid system to improve its economic growth and to achieve long-term sustainability. Let us begin by exploring Venezuela's inherited economy.

The Inherited Economy

Critics of Hugo Chavez and the Chavian Revolution who focus on the negative aspects of the Venezuelan economy and social system, such as the fact that there is high unemployment rate, should understand that Chavez inherited a country that has been facing capital flight for the last two decades, and that he was not the first President to apply exchange controls to stabilize the bolivar and the economy. Venezuela was also under the influence of IMF policies in the past, which resulted in worse living conditions. The country also faced an oil strike by the business elites during 2002-2003, which crippled the economy for a short time, but is now back on track profiting from the high cost of crude oil. The policies of Chavez's government is to repair damages that resulted from past policies and those that are deem not within the interest of the people, such as economic liberalization, privatization, deregulation, and foreign investors.

Venezuela faced capital flight in 1982 and then again in 1994. It reached historical levels during 1982 when U.S. $8 billion left the country. The state oil company was forced to "repatriate foreign reserves in an attempt to shore up the domestic currency."[139] In 1983, President Luis Herrera Campins (1979 – 1984) "imposed a tiered system of exchange controls with the cheapest rate – for the import of essential goods – set at 7 bolivars to the dollar," up from 4.3 bolivars to the dollar. This made debt repayments difficult. Corruption also cost the country U.S. $11 billion in foreign reserves.[140]

Capital flight in 1982 was not the only thing that had a negative impact on the country. The other is IMF structural adjustment policy. In 1988, President Carlos Andrews Perez handed the country over to them. This meant the privatization of businesses, cuts in public spending, liberalization, and deregulation. This resulted in an economic contraction of 8.6%. Poverty increased from 43.9% in 1988 to 66.5% in 1989.

There was another major capital flight in 1994 due to a large banking crisis. The President at that time was Rafael Caldera. Inflation was 70.8% due to the devaluation of the currency. Price exchange control was imposed and another U.S. $1.4 billion IMF loan was negotiated in 1995. Poverty kept rising despite the fact that there was an increase in foreign investments and a rise in oil prices.

The economy took another major downturn during the 2002-2003 oil strike at the state oil company Petroleos de Venezuela (PDVSA), which has been accused of being led by the executives there and the business elite in the country. The oil sector lost U.S. $3.7 billion and the non-oil sector lost $1.19 billion as a result of the strike. Foreign reserves decreased to U.S. $11.05 billion on January 20, 2003 from $11.93 billion at the beginning of the year. The purpose of having foreign reserves is to act as a buffer against the flight of money. The government acted quickly and implemented price control. In January, 2003, the auction of dollars was

---

[139] Julia Buxton, "Economic Policy and the Rise of Hugo Chavez", in Steve Ellner and Daniel Hellinger, eds., *Venezuelan Politics in Chavez Era* (Lynner Rienner Publishers, 2003).

[140] Ibid.

suspended in order to stabilize the bolivar. A $2,000 a year spending limit was imposed upon those who travel abroad. The finance ministry issued billions of dollars worth of bonds to the general public as a way for them to get around the price controls. Financial institutions are limited to 20% of the $1 billion dollar in bonds that were initially issued, and each financial institution is capped off at $50 million. This is a smart move by the government to prevent institutional investors from causing fluctuations of the bolivar if and when they choose to sell off the bonds. The ten month long currency control was deemed affective. The finance ministry estimated that foreign reserves at the end of 2003 stands at $20.7 billion, an increase of $9 billion or 30% since the middle of January, 2003. As of May 7, 2007, foreign reserves stand at $24.6 billion.[141]

Price control during these times of crisis helps to stabilize the country, but much more is being done these days by the Chavez government to rid of negative foreign influence such as IMF policies and also to get rid of poverty and increase social utility. Let us begin by exploring why the country is defying the FTAA (Free Trade Area of the Americas) and adopting ALBA (Bolivarian Alternative for Latin American and the Caribbean) in its place.

Against the FTAA

FTAA "responds to the interest of transnational capital and pursues absolute liberalization of trade in goods, services and investments...."[142] The negotiating process of FTAA is undemocratic and not transparent. "The privatization of services is a death knell for the people across the region."[143] Rights would go to corporations instead of the people. On the other hand, the purpose of ALBA is to fight poverty and is against social exclusion. It is based on a compensatory fund, which corrects the

---

[141] "Venezuelan Foreign Reserves Fall Sharply" (Associated Press), Friday, May 11, 2007. Article available at http://in.us.biz.yahoo.com/ap/070511/venezuela_reserves.html?.v=1

[142] Venezuela Analysis, available at http://www.venezuelanalysis.com, Thursday, February 5, 2004.

[143] Ibid.

disparities between the economically weaker countries and the main economic powers. One of the prime directives of ALBA is endogenous development, or development from within the region, which lacks diversification of production. FTAA cannot achieve this goal in which "economic growth is in harmony with increasing quality of life and higher degree of well-being" for the people of Latin America, especially when it involves the "industrial sweatshops and extensive exploitation of the work force."[144] The alternative proposal is based on solidarity. In order to correct the asymmetries between the advantaged from the disadvantage, changes within the nature of competition must occur in addition to having solidarity between the people and the governments.

Venezuela's position on the FTAA mirrors their social movement critique in its Constitution. What the government wants is more equality between countries, national sovereignty, and people's rights to education, health care, and food security. The policy of the FTAA does not aim for these things.

On the issue of national sovereignty, the FTAA aims to reduce state control over domestic policymaking. Foreign capital increases its control over the local economy. Venezuela argues that "the state must maintain a role in promoting domestic economic development through [the] use of national resources and state contracts, including tools as technology transfer and performance requirement."[145] They are against foreign ownership of domestic businesses and government procurement.

The Venezuelan government is against privatization, including the privatization of education. According to the Constitution, all citizens are guaranteed full and free access to education. "Missions" have been set up to provide free education at the primary, secondary, and higher levels. One such mission is Mission Robinson, which is a literacy program aimed at educating over 1 million illiterate adults. Thousands of new elementary schools have been built for the poor, including a recently built university for students who cannot get into the exclusive ones due to a lack of space.

In addition to free education, people have a right to free health care, which is more important than patent rights of the FTAA. Through the Barrior Andentor program, Cuban doctors are placed in the poor

---

[144] Ibid.

[145] Venezuela Analysis, Monday, February 23, 2004.

neighborhoods of Caracas to provide service for the disadvantaged. Cuban doctors are brought over due to the lack of doctors in the country. In return, Cuba gets subsidized oil. Since healthcare is a basic and necessary right, the government grants compulsory licenses to national companies to produce generic versions of patented medicines and also foods.

The priority of moving the country away from oil exports and into sustainable agriculture is outlined in Article 304 of the Constitution. "Venezuela called for the reduction of protectionist export subsidies of rich countries to support their agricultural sections to preserve food sovereignty, cultural diversity, and traditional rural livelihoods."[146] The government is also against bio-piracy and seed patenting because it believes that the indigenous people and the peasants have the right to "protect their traditional knowledge" and farmers have the right to "protect and utilize the seeds that they themselves produce."[147]

These are some of the reasons why Venezuela is against FTAA. They value the right to basic necessities over corporate profits. Let us now examine how the government is further protecting the rights of its people and increasing social utility by examining other ways that it is increasing its control of its economy.

Increasing Control over the Economy

Venezuela is actively increasing its control over the private sectors. The government is limiting and in some cases totally excluding foreign investors and business owners. One such policy is the limitation of foreign mining to place state control over natural resources.[148] The government believes that nationalization of the mining industry including other industries will "tackle poverty and boost growth."[149] The government

---

[146] Ibid.

[147] Ibid.

[148] BBC News, September 22, 2005.

[149] Ibid.

claims that foreign-owned business "have taken profits out of the country and contributed to high levels of poverty."[150]

Another sector the government is exerting control over is the financial sector. The government insists that private banks appoint two state representatives to their board.[151] The Central Bank has also set limits on interest rates.[152] As of May 1, 2005, annual interest rates for loans are capped off at 28 percent, and private banks must pay at least 6.5 percent interest on deposits. Chavez argues that banks should offer lower interest rates to the poor. This policy will also result in banks having stricter policies on loans. Higher interest rates on deposits should help encourage savings. Critics would argue that in order to stimulate the economy, it would be necessary to keep interest rates low from time to time to stimulate spending and borrowing. However, for the time being, the government has all the money it needs from high oil prices. Let us now explore PDVSA, the state's oil company, which is the financial engine behind the social revolution.

Petro de Venezuela: The Engine Behind the Social Revolution

Venezuela has 80 billion proven barrels of oil reserves.[153] In fact, the government's main source of revenue is from Petroleos de Venezuela (PDVSA), the state owned oil company, which has estimated revenues of $75 billion for 2005. Four billion of internal budget went to social programs and projects like highways and railways. "Nearly $10 billion more flows into the Venezuelan treasury, forming the backing – 35% - of the federal budget."[154] For this reason, PDVSA is the engine behind the social revolution.

---

[150] Ibid.

[151] BBC News, September 2, 2005.

[152] Associated Press, April 28, 2005.

[153] See "Crude Realities: Living with Chavez, Oil's New Mr. Big," *Fortune*, Monday, September 19, 2005.

[154] Ibid.

Venezuela is a major supplier of oil to the U.S. About 50% of Venezuela's oil is exported to the U.S. to be exact. In the first half of 2005, it provided a seventh of U.S. oil imports, or 1.6 million barrels a day. Chavez threatens to stop exports to the U.S. if they challenge Caracas. Critics would argue that both countries are dependent upon each other – the U.S. as the largest buyer and Venezuela as a major supplier. But it is not true that Venezuela has to rely upon the U.S. because there are other major oil hungry countries out there that Venezuela can sell to, such as China with its robust economy.

Rafael Ramirez, the Energy Minister and CEO of PDVSA, lays out the goals of the company during an interview with *Fortune Magazine*.[155] These goals are aimed against foreign companies profiting from Venezuela's oil market and they are to also increase government control and influence over the global market. Goal 1: Impose higher taxes on royalties to help fund social programs. Taxes are set at 50%, up from 34%. Royalties increased to 17% on each barrel from 1%. The government is insisting on joint ventures rather than operating agreements, with Venezuela controlling at least 51% of the company. Ramirez argues, "When the private companies have control over production, it's impossible to conduct your own national oil policy," hence the need for the state's control over its oil market. Goal 2: He wants other nationals oil companies (NOCs) such as those in Iran and Saudia Arabia to work with PDVSA to wrestle power away from private companies such as Exxon. Goal 3: He wants PDVSA to be more influential in OPEC. Venezuela was a founding member and it is the biggest non-Arab member. Let us now explore what the revenues from PDVSA have done for Venezuela.

Social Achievements and Economic Growth

One of the social achievements of the Chavian Revolution is the establishment of "missions".[156] The Constitution guarantees free access to education, healthcare, and other basic necessities. Mission Ribas provides free high school education, which includes food, accommodation and

---

[155] Ibid.

[156] See "The Fight against Poverty", *Venezuela Analysis*, Monday, July 4, 2005.

travel expenses. On June 1, 2005, 20,686 people have graduated from these schools. Chavez has decided to increase the budget for Mission Ribas by $50 million per month. A similar mission is Mission Sucre, which provides free college education. By the end of 2005, 210,000 people graduate from college. Mission Barrior Adentro provides free healthcare to the people of Venezuela. It is support by more than 20,000 Cuban doctors. The reason why Cuban doctors are brought in is because there is a lack of Venezuelan doctors to meet the needs of patients. This mission resulted in over 184 million consultations and saved more than 25,000 lives. Last, but not least is Mission Mercal, or subsidized supermarkets. Over 25,000 of these supermarkets exist and they capture 60% of the overall food market. They sell food up to 50% cheaper than private, capitalist chains. Mission Mercal was prompted by the 2002 – 2003 oil strike, which resulted in severe shortage of food and other basic necessities. The program has been boosted by $295 million of additional funding to expand existing outlets and to create another 1,000 food houses to provide for the very poor.

The government also spent money on infrastructure development since Chavez came into power.[157] The national railroad network has been restarted. It has also carried out construction of subway systems, bridges, damns, highways, and other projects.

Economic data shows positive results for Venezuela including poverty and unemployment being lower in 2005, high currency reserves, a decreased level in country-risk, high savings, and a strong stock market. According to Venezuela's National Institute of Statistics (INE), poverty was estimated to drop 8% points at the end of 2005, or to 35%, down from 47% in 2004.[158] "Critical poverty, the level at which people cannot afford to cover their basic needs, dropped to 10.1% in the first half of 2005, down from 18% the previous year."[159] Unemployment is down to 11.5% in September, 2005 from 14.5% the same time in 2004. The decrease of poverty and unemployment has been linked to the strong growth of the economy, which grew consecutively for the past seven quarters. It grew

---

[157] See Ibid., "A Venezuelan Miracle?", Tuesday, February 3, 2004.

[158] See Ibid., "Poverty and Unemployment Down in 2005", Friday, October 14, 2005.

[159] Ibid.

17% in 2004, relative to the prior year. In the first quarter of 2005, the economy grew by 7.5%, and then 11.1% in the second quarter.

The country's high currency reserves and low country-risk gives it a strong and stable financial base. The "international currency reserve figure is similar to the total external debt of the country" and this is "something that is unimaginable for any other Latin American country, and which shows an undeniable solidity in terms of the country's guarantee with regard to its financial commitments."[160] The country-risk indicator EMB+[3] lowered to 596 base points on December 22, 2003 from 1406 base points in February, 2003. This drop of 812 points means that the country pays 8.1% less in interest rates when it needs to borrow from the international market.

High savings and a strong stock market are also positive economic signs. Ten trillion bolivars of liquidity are in saving accounts. This is a significant number when we compare it to the government budget of 40 trillion bolivars. This is due to currency controls, which reduced capital flight. The Caracas Stock Exchange increased from 6,780.78 in March, 2002 to 27,531 in December, 2004, which is over a 300% increase. It stands at roughly 38,900 as of May 6, 2007.[161]

Despite all the social achievements, infrastructure development, and economic growth, there is still room for improvement. Let us now explore these and also some of the criticisms against Chaves and his government.

Room for Improvement and Learning from China

There is plenty of room for improvement. Certain policies would run counter to Chavez's stance on socialism, while others are not. The first area that can be improved is the states' oil company. Despite PDVSA's massive profits, critics have argued that the company needs to invest in more projects. The government has an over reliance on oil exports to fund its treasury and social programs. "Any sudden downturn in oil prices cannot be offset by a commensurate increase in production, which leaves

---

[160] "A Venezuelan Miracle?"

[161] The Caracas Stock Exchange, or Bolsa de Valores de Caracas, at http://www.bolsadecaracas.com/esp/index.jsp.

the government's revenue base vulnerable."[162] Due to the nationalization and Chavez's anti-capitalist stance, foreign investment has nearly halted except the oil, gas and a few correlated industries. The same source also mentioned about capital flight despite the contrary reports. The source states that money continues leaving the country and that the "business community operates with a short term mindset, ready to pack up and leave if and when the economy collapses."[163]

Another area Venezuela can improve upon is public investment to create new jobs. James Petras criticized the government's policy during the "Defense of Humanity" conference held during December 1-5, 2004 in Caracas. The government should not depend upon the private sector to generate employment because they are doing so for credits and incentives. "They are not [willing] to [make] large-scale long-term investments necessary" through public works.[164] Petras argues that the government should tackle the root of the problem, which is to provide "well-paying, stable jobs, so that social services improve people's lives, rather than being substituted for the structure changes necessary for them to have a decent life...."[165]

Petras' argument is partly against socialism. Providing incentives or subsidy to the private sector can and has often resulted in less productivity and innovation. Critics of the Venezuelan government and against socialism in general would argue that markets should be open to allow room for competition. Competition will lead to greater productivity and innovation. It will also lead to lower cost of goods and services. They will also argue that more jobs will be generated by welcoming foreign investment and foreign business owners. Chavez's view on this is that he criticizes foreign businesses for taking money out of the country, which is why he limits foreign entities and nationalizing many sectors. He believes

---

[162] See "Failed promise of neo-liberal policies has tilted the region to the left: South American's Balancing Act: Socialism vs. Fiscal Conservatism", *Noticas Fianciera / Groupo de Diarios America*, May 20, 2005.

[163] Ibid.

[164] "Weighing the Revolution: The Limits of Social Spending, the Need for Structural Change in Venezuela", *Venezuela Analysis* at http://www.venezuelanalysis.com, Monday, December 6, 2004.

[165] Ibid.

that this will allow his government to have greater control of its domestic policies, and thus its future, and all of this is in the interest of the people instead of for corporate profit. Even though the government has a constant stream of revenue from the oil sector, it does not mean that they cannot make improvements upon the social structure and economy, with the intention of increasing overall social utility and long-term stability. There are critics who will argue that Venezuela should learn from China's successful policies, which we will now explore.

China is ruled by a communist party and their economic system is more capitalistic than socialistic. The challenge for the Chinese Communist Party is to maintain popular support and at the same time adopt the free-market system and decentralization. The reason they adopted the latter elements is to avoid making the same mistake like the former Soviet Union. China's economy has grown tremendously since the mid to early 1980's as a result of adopting the standard free market system. This includes the privatization of businesses, including ones that the state used to monopolize. One such industry is the telecommunications industry. The majority of the population is employed by state owned companies, but this is slowly decreasing. The dilemma is that many of these state owned enterprises (SOEs) are not making profit, but they are kept afloat for the sole reason of providing jobs. If unemployment is too high, the communist party might lose support and it may also cause social turmoil. It is, however, not within China's long-term interest to do this because it costs the state a lot of money. It would be more productive for them to privatize these companies and to invest in the public sector to generate more jobs. They have already begun doing this, and due to the tremendous growth of the economy and cities, especially along the coast where the trade ports are located, many new employment opportunities have arisen. There have also been many employment opportunities for the migrant workers (those migrating to the urban areas from the rural areas to find work) in construction. This is due to the large population migration into the urban areas resulting in the construction of housing units and infrastructure projects like highways. China has also opened up their markets to foreigners and also encourages foreign direct investment. It is now one of the leading competitors in the world market thanks to the low cost of production. China also conducts major trade with other countries, especially with the U.S.

China's major growth can be found in its economic data. *Chinadaily* reports that the economy is predicted to grow at the rate of 8% per year for the next five years. Economic output should reach $2.6 trillion by 2010.[166] For the first 11 months of 2004, its trade volume was over US $1 trillion, an increase of 36% over the previous year.[167] In 2004, bilateral trade with North America was over US $167 billion, with Europe, over US $190 billion, and with Asia, over US $600 billion. China is also becoming a leader in electronic equipment. The trade volume in electromechanical and hi-tech products in 2004 was US $700 billion. Foreign direct invest has also increased in China. In 2004, contractual foreign investment surpassed US $1 trillion. Those in the high-teach industry grew by a large margin, and 700 foreign investment centers were established, mostly in the electronics and the communications industry. Multinational corporations have 30 regional headquarters in China. All of this is a sign of China's rapid growing economy and huge labor market, and this is why it would be mistake for other countries such as the U.S. to not invest in China.

The result of China's growth is due to its economic liberalization and decentralization, and all of this is done with the Chinese Communist Party still in control. Some critics out there would argue that Chavez should take the same approach. The purpose in doing so is to make Venezuela's economic system grow and to provide long-term, stable, and well paying jobs for the population. Venezuela can continue to fund its social programs. On the surface, it looks good, but certain things are lacking if there is too much state welfare, such as a lack of productivity, innovation, and self-sufficiency.

Conclusion

Venezuela has shown tremendous economic growth and social improvement since the reign of Hugo Chavez and the Chavian Revolution. This, however, does not mean that the government should not learn affective policies of other countries. It is fine to put the interests of the

---

[166] *China Daily* at http://www.chinadaily.com, February 11, 2005.

[167] "Minister Bo Xilai: The Commercial Undertaking Will Keep a Good Momentum Steady Progress Next Year", December 30, 2004, from the Network Center of MOFCOM.

people first, but it is a mistake for the state to act as a long-term crutch for the people because the people and businesses would not be self-sufficient. The long-term interest and not the short-term interest of the economy and of society should be the primary concern. Chavez will also have to devise a plan to ensure a strong, effective, and stable government, and this is also within the long-term interest of the country. We do not know how long Chavez will stay in office and how long this social revolution will last. The next President may not be as popular with the people or as effective as Chavez. I suggest that the planning and implementation of social, economic, and political policies be made with a broader and a longer time horizon in mind. It is logically possible for Venezuela to come up with a hybrid system that has the interests of the people as being primary, but also one that would allow rapid development and long-term sustainability. If Chavez wants to set an example of an alternative system for others to follow, he must not only take care of its people, but also take steps to ensure that Venezuela will have highly skilled workers and a market that can compete on the international level.

LaVergne, TN USA
06 April 2011
223007LV00001B/14/P